Reversing Degenerative Disease offers a message of hope and a blueprint for wellness. Anyone interested in mind, body and spiritual health should read this book.

—WAYNE M. SOTILE, PH.D.
AUTHOR, *THRIVING WITH HEART DISEASE*

Excellent book! Finally, encouragement for patients with degenerative diseases. Health is in your hands; you can get better, and this book tells you how.

—DR. JESSICA DIETRICH

Dr. Elrod has a refreshing workable approach to total health and wellness with an emphasis on the power of a positive mental and spiritual attitude.

—HEIDI ELROD RICHARDSON, L.M.T.

This book will not only help your body, but also your mind and soul. May God bless Dr. Elrod's efforts.

—JOEY HIDOCK, PGA MEMBER
MASTER MODELGOLF.COM INSTRUCTOR

The Bible makes it clear that overall good health is God's will. Dr. Joe Elrod has incorporated the natural side of medical and physiological health with sound Bible principles. His insight is both refreshing and enlightening.

—SCOTT WEBB, PASTOR
WORD OF LIFE CHRISTIAN CENTER
BIRMINGHAM, AL

REVERSING

DEGENERATIVE DISEASE

JOE M. ELROD, ED.D.

SILOAM®
A STRANG COMPANY

REVERSING DEGENERATIVE DISEASE by Joe M. Elrod, Ed.D.
Published by Siloam
A Strang Company
600 Rinehart Road
Lake Mary, Florida 32746
www.siloam.com

Cover design by Eric Powell

This book is not intended to provide medical advice or to take the place of medical advice and treatment from your personal physician. Readers are advised to consult their own doctors or other qualified health professionals regarding the treatment of their medical problems. Neither the publisher nor the author takes any responsibility for any possible consequences from any treatment, action or preparation to any person reading or following the information in this book. If readers are taking prescription medications, they should consult with

their physicians and not take themselves off of medicines to start supplementation without the proper supervision of a physician.

Library of Congress Cataloging-in-Publication Data

Elrod, Joe M.
  Reversing degenerative disease / Joe M. Elrod.
    p. cm.
  ISBN 0-88419-946-0 (Tradepaper)
  1. Naturopathy. 2. Degeneration (Pathology)—Alternative treat-
  ment. 3. Chronic diseases—Alternative treatment. 4. Self-care,
  Health. I. Title.
RZ440.E44 2003
615.5'35—dc21

                        2003001555

03 04 05 06 07 — 87654321
Printed in the United States of America

This work is gratefully and respectfully dedicated to

PATTI

...for her untiring assistance, creativity and invaluable input
that add tremendously to this book. As a result of her
touch and help with content, format, sequence and flow,
the lives of many who read this book will be impacted in
a much greater way. Without her total support and loyalty
that allowed me to do the things I needed to do, this project
could not have been completed in this timely fashion.

...for her heart, desire and passion to give to others and
help them find God's pathway for healing...to help them
move away from pain, heartache, misery and broken spirits.

...for her awareness that our Creator has a special
blueprint and purpose for each life...to assist readers
in discovering God's peace, joy and abundance for
their lives...and more importantly, to assist them
in discovering God's purpose for them in this world.

...for her gift of counseling and encouragement
that she uses so extraordinarily well.

I praise my Creator for His perfect timing in sending my true
soul mate and perfect life partner who shares equally our
vision, mission, passion and ministry.

ACKNOWLEDGMENTS

I thank God for leading me to Siloam, the Christian health imprint for Strang Communications, and opening a dimension of my life that has blessed me in a way that is truly overwhelming. God's nature and grace are incomprehensible, and I am so very thankful.

As this challenging endeavor draws near to the final stage, it is both heartwarming and comforting to think of all those who have been helpful, supportive, encouraging and inspiring. One of God's most wonderful promises is that once a heart's desire is born, if it is good and in His purpose, He will provide the people and resources to bring it about for the good of all.

I would now like to express thanks and appreciation for all those who have directly or indirectly assisted me in formulating and expressing the information, research and knowledge expressed on the pages of this book.

- Stephen Strang, founder and president of Strang Communications—for your vision and faith to serve as God's point man to bring about this anointed publishing house.

- Dave Welday—for your continuous encouragement and faith in me, and your belief that this project is worthy of making a difference for those suffering from degenerative disease.

- Tom Marin—who came into the game in the fourth quarter, bringing talent, experience and enthusiasm that add greatly to the quality and success of this creation.

- Barbara Dycus—our esteemed managing editor who took a major interest in this work and offered invaluable assistance in its restructuring and formatting.

- Carol Noe—the one who has directed and nurtured this project from day one, the one who first believed that I could make a contribution as a Siloam author. Your work ethic, devotion to detail and commitment to our project is unsurpassed and forever appreciated. Your creativity and editorial skills are second to none.

- Ann Mulchan—our all-pro liaison who provided the continuous excellence of connecting the parts that expedited the process daily, always in a most gracious, caring manner.

- Atalie Anderson—for your invaluable assistance and gracious attention to detail and forever being Carol's faithful girl Friday.

- The visionary people at Strang Communications and Siloam—for your enthusiasm and passion for this book and its author. All those wonderful, talented people throughout the publishing house family, too numerous to name, all the specialized departments that bring it together behind the scenes, that offer gracious and tireless support and attention to the details on a challenging schedule that brought us to completion through a fabulous team effort—Godspeed to all of you.

- Dale Wilstermann and Woodley Auguste—for your warmth, diligence and enthusiastic efforts in your astute preparation for marketing and promotion to reach the millions that are seeking answers and hope for their health dilemmas that impact their lives, marriages and families.

- Dr. Jim Hill—a valued friend and esteemed colleague, one of the true pioneers who has been

diligent in helping to blaze the trail in complementary and alternative medicine. Always there
for his friends, clients and patients, he has a heart
for God with a mission to reach and help those in
need.

• The numerous hospitals, medical centers, univer-
sities, professional associations, foundations, individual chiropractors, physicians, naturopaths and
health practitioners that continue to initiate and
sponsor educational forums and events that help
degenerative disease patients and their families
worldwide.

• My wonderful staff, colleagues and associates at
The Body Advantage, Inc.—for creating the most
stimulating and rewarding, yet warm and supportive, environment that any professional family
ever called home.

• All my students, patients, clients, readers and
fellow professionals—who number in the hundreds
of thousands, who have taught me and inspired me
more than I could ever return in two lifetimes.

• Dr. Jack Nelson—my esteemed and talented
major professor who possesses a gift for making
you think you are more than you are. An accomplished professor and author who first inspired me
to think that one day I could make an impact on
others' lives through research and writing.

• Dr. Francis Drury—my department chair at
Louisiana State University, a visionary who quietly
made a difference and is responsible for pushing
me to greater heights and expanding my vision,
who gave me the invaluable awareness of the power
of the subconscious mind and positive thinking.

• Beth Mitchell—led to the Body Advantage
family through a divine appointment; truly a god-
send. Your invaluable literary skills and gracious
devotion and assistance to this anointed project

were critical, especially during several deadline crunch times.

- Destiny Dawn Broome Harris (Brent)—always faithful and gracious for providing the little extras with a smile when most needed. You bring a breath of warmth, fresh air and grace to my life. Then Brandon, Whitney and Brad, as promised in Ephesians, blessings beyond what we can ask or think.

- Katherine DeLise Elrod McCorkle (Bill), my first-born—your pure heart, your love for our Lord Jesus Christ, your gracious nature and the way you use your gift of caring and encouragement for your family, friends, community, church and all those with whom you come in contact are a great inspiration to me daily without your knowing. I am so very thankful to be called "Daddy" by you.

- Will, Katherine Elizabeth, and Brockie—pieces of my heart.

- Heidi Jo Elrod Richardson (Ben), my baby daughter—your smile, your sense of humor and ability to make me and others laugh, your physical and inner beauty, your incredible people skills, your awesome voice and your extraordinary gift with children are all so awe inspiring for me. I love your faith and visionary nature, which I taught you and we so thankfully share. You motivate me daily to move forward and create materials that impact the quality of others' lives. I am so very thankful to be your "Daddy."

- Clarkie—a piece of my heart.

CONTENTS

FOREWORD

It has been my pleasure to be acquainted with Dr. Joe Elrod on a personal level for the past two years. However, I first became aware of Dr. Elrod's work in 1997 when I used his book *Reversing Fibromyalgia* as one of my main references for my Ph.D. thesis.

Since then I have become most impressed with Dr. Elrod's approach to degenerative diseases. In the pages of this book, Dr. Elrod offers a comprehensive health protocol to help many who struggle with various diseases and illnesses. Dr. Elrod's proven protocol will make a wonderful difference in the lives of those who commit to follow it.

Clearly, Dr. Elrod's research and work merit the respect of all those involved in healthcare. This is a must-read book for anyone who has or knows of anyone with a degenerative disease. His compassion and sincerity for individuals who suffer from degenerative disease can be felt on every page.

I am grateful to have the ability to use Dr. Elrod's protocol in my natural health practice, and I hope that my colleagues will find the protocols to be equally beneficial in their practice.

—JIMMIE D. HILL, N.D., PH.D.
NATURAL HEALTH CONSULTANT

INTRODUCTION

The Toxicity, Aging and Disease Connection

Only recently has the connection between toxicity, aging and disease been established and more widely recognized. Even so, I have spent my entire career as an academician, research scientist and author searching for ways to prevent and reverse the ill effects of the havoc toxicity causes that wreck human health and well-being.

It is personally satisfying to know that there is a growing consensus among research scientists and academicians, as well as medical experts, of the causal relationship between inflammation (free-radical damage) created by toxicity and many chronic degenerative diseases. Incredibly, this list of degenerative diseases includes atherosclerosis, diabetes, fibromyalgia, osteoporosis, cancer, heart disease, lupus, irritable bowel syndrome and arthritis. Even more common maladies such as back pain, chronic stiffness, headaches (including migraines), colds, flu and other viruses, which are the result of a compromised immune system, relate to the connection between toxicity, aging and disease.

DEVELOPMENT OF A HEALTH THEORY

After completing doctoral studies at Louisiana State University, I lived in the real world for a few years, enjoying my position as a young university professor. From what I observed during those years, I questioned more and more the conventional wisdom of our medical healthcare system. I began to refer to it as our disease care system instead, since we seem to wait until we become ill before thinking about our health. Then, instead of trying to eliminate our illness by treating the cause, our medical approach is simply to mask the symptoms of illness, using prescription drugs and other conventional methods intended to make us more comfortable with the illness.

My consternation over this ineffective approach to medical treatment inspired me to challenge conventional thinking and to begin a search for alternative methods that would bring healing. As an exercise physiologist, my education had given me a tremendous advantage over conventional medical students because of the depth of study required and the knowledge I had gained in the areas of nutrition and exercise, which are not typically offered to medical students.

In my search for answers to a growing health crisis, I began to read the works of pioneers in the field of alternative medicine like Linus Pauling, who developed theories of the healing power of vitamin C, and Adele Davis, who became a renowned nutritionist during the 1960s. The powerful works of Paavo Airola and Dr. Andrew Weil have been especially inspiring in the area of alternative healing.

In addition to these studies, I began to contemplate the great benefits I have personally enjoyed in my overall health from a lifestyle of exercise. I feel extremely fortunate that I have had the opportunity to be an athlete and a "fitness buff" my entire life. This has enabled me to build and maintain muscular strength, flexibility and cardiovascular efficiency; I have enjoyed wellness and a high quality of life for sixty years. My desire to help people enjoy health keeps me exposed to situations of illness that make me realize what a wonderful blessing my health is. It has been my joy to be able to make a difference for many people, guiding them to a much healthier and better quality of life.

What happened to our nutrition?

For generations preceding us, the soil has been depleted of its nutrients. We have not been kind enough to allow it to replenish itself, as the Bible taught us we need to do. Thousands of years ago, Scripture taught us the wisdom of allowing the soil to rest:

> Six years you shall sow your land and gather in its produce, but the seventh year you shall let it rest and lie fallow, that the poor of your people may eat; and what they leave, the beasts of the field may eat. In like manner you shall do with your vineyard and your olive grove.
>
> —*Exodus 23:10–11*

For almost a century now we have been producing foods artificially with chemicals such as herbicides, pesticides, insecticides and fertilizers. When I became aware of this practice twenty-five years ago, I understood that the food we were producing did not have the nutrients our bodies need for health, and I began to study the world of natural supplements that could make up for this lack. I learned about vitamins, minerals, herbs and special nutrients such as coenzyme Q_{10}, grape seed extract and apple cider vinegar. I became convinced that natural supplements are beneficial to health and well-being, and I began taking them personally. Gradually, I began to realize even greater personal health, and you will see results of my experiences and research reflected throughout this book as a part of my protocol.

I began to incorporate my personal experience with nutritional supplements into my teaching, research and development of health and wellness programs. When I investigated a disease process, I was challenged to find new, alternative, natural therapies that would complement traditional treatments. As I continued to improve my personal health habits because of my research, my immune system became even stronger. I began to realize that my body was working more efficiently than ever. The two major changes I made personally were to improve my eating habits and to begin taking natural supplements.

During my years in graduate study and continuing into my early years as a professor and research scientist, I began to make some revealing connections between disease, aging and a compromised immune system. It was alarming to observe the obvious consequences that resulted from weakening our immune systems, and my concern inspired me to pursue my studies. Since I believed that toxicity, disrupted sleep patterns and damaged immune systems were the basis of ill health and disease, my mission became to find alternative methods to prevent, treat and reverse the symptoms safely.

Two realms of healing

My personal experience that involved me in pursuing answers to disease and illness soon brought me to the realization that the Creator gives us two realms within which to operate: the natural and the supernatural. I also understood that God expects us to grasp the faith that operates in both of these realms. His Word is filled with wonderful promises for those who obey His commands that pertain to our health:

> If you diligently heed the voice of the LORD your God and
> do what is right in His sight, give ear to His commandments

and keep all His statutes, I will put none of the diseases on
you which I have brought on the Egyptians. For I am the
Lord who heals you.

—Exodus 15:26

This is only one of the many promises of healing expressed by
God in His living Word. Pay particular attention to the fact that the
promise is written in the present tense, for the here and now. God
declared, "I am the Lord who *heals* you." God is—forever and continuously—our healer. However, this promise is conditional; it begins
with the little word *if* that introduces the condition of obedience.

The condition God sets out is that we must give our best effort
in following His principles for a good life. When we strive to meet
the conditions, the promise of health and abundance is ours.
Scripture declares the unchangeableness of God, so what the biblical
writers conveyed to us over two thousand years ago regarding the
promises of God still stands firm today. (See Hebrews 13:8.)

According to the testimony of Scripture, God can heal us
instantaneously. But He also makes provision for healing as a
process over time as we utilize the miracles of medical science and
the natural resources or alternative measures. God would prefer that
we not get sick; it is His will that we be healthy and prosperous.
(See 3 John 2.)

Your quest for renewed health

Would you believe me if I told you that you can regain vital
health in just twelve weeks? It is everyone's desire to be pain free and
energetic, to sleep peacefully, to have a toned, healthy body and to
feel good about yourself. Most people desire to enjoy more success
with family, friendships and personal and business endeavors. All that
is possible if you are willing to consider seriously the health protocols discussed in this book.

If you will make a firm, positive decision to change your life forever, I will make a commitment to be your mentor, your "success
coach," if you will. Remember also, as you make your decision, that
you have the great Healer (God) on your side, desiring the best for
you. During your twelve-week commitment, I will provide for you in
this book the natural protocols (gifts of God) that promote and restore
health. And our great Healer will be faithful to add supernaturally
what you need to help you along your pathway of healing. All you
need to do is to believe God's loving promises for your health and

claim them for your own. He will help you to make permanent lifestyle changes as well to ensure continued health. One of my favorite promises reads:

> If God is for us, who can be against us? He who did not spare His own Son, but delivered Him up for us all, how shall He not with Him also freely give us all things?
>
> —*Romans 8:31–32*

A unique and scientific program

This unique and scientifically proven twelve-week program has been developed out of twenty years of research along with "hands-on" experience with literally thousands of readers and patients around the world. (See Part IV for details.) Over the past several years I have personally worked with men and women of all ages (specifically ages nine to ninety-four), helping them to implement the program.

I rejoice in the fact that I have received calls from England, Australia, Canada, Mexico and throughout the United States from people who have benefited from my program. They tell me that after completing the program, they now have their lives back, pain and symptom free.

It has been especially heartwarming to witness lives, marriages and families being restored to health. I received a call one day in my office from a grandmother in North Carolina. Her first words were, "Thank you for giving me my life back." Then she described how she could pick up her grandbaby once again. What a joy it was for me to get such a report from one who had suffered from a degenerative disease to the extent that she was bedridden and is now well after following my program.

Over the years, many physicians, chiropractors and therapists who were trained in the traditional programs have chosen to utilize my alternative program in their practices and have done so successfully. Please refer to the simple diagram on the next page that shows that disease and ill health cannot exist when seven factors are present. Good health involves a comprehensive approach to ensure that the body, mind and spirit are receiving all they need to experience it.

ILLUSTRATION OF THE RESULTS OF
DR. ELROD'S BODY ADVANTAGE
PROGRAM AND PROTOCOL

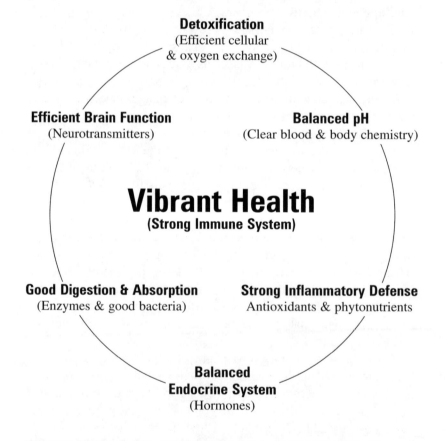

Detoxification
(Efficient cellular
& oxygen exchange)

Efficient Brain Function
(Neurotransmitters)

Balanced pH
(Clear blood & body chemistry)

Vibrant Health
(Strong Immune System)

Good Digestion & Absorption
(Enzymes & good bacteria)

Strong Inflammatory Defense
Antioxidants & phytonutrients

**Balanced
Endocrine System**
(Hormones)

WHEN THESE FACTORS ARE PRESENT
DISEASE AND ILL HEALTH CANNOT EXIST

Just do it!

One simple evidence of your desire to be well is that you are reading this book. If you will allow me, I will teach you how to invest less than 10 percent of your time in such a way that it will bring extraordinary changes to your body, your mind and your self-esteem, and impact all areas of your life for the better.

I will outline and help you to plan every step of the process. I'll help you stay on track and bounce back from setbacks, and I will give you encouragement when you need it the most and be a positive force in assisting you in realizing your fullest potential. The good news is that you can be well and enjoy the benefits of a strong, healthy body without starving yourself. In this program, you will learn how to tone and lose fat while eating well and enjoying healthful food.

> **You absolutely can accomplish whatever you set your mind to—no matter if you are nine or ninety-four, male or female, healthy or unhealthy, suffering a degenerative disease or other systemic ailment.**

Imagine waking in the morning, fully rested, full of energy and really excited about the person you see in the mirror. Go ahead and visualize three months from now, a new you, with energy, health and confidence to accomplish whatever you set your mind to do. You absolutely can accomplish whatever you set your mind to—no matter if you are nine or ninety-four, male or female, healthy or unhealthy, suffering a degenerative disease or other systemic ailment.

The first step to receiving help is to ask for it. God has promised to respond to us when we reach out to Him and ask:

> So I say to you, ask, and it will be given to you; seek, and
> you will find; knock, and it will be opened to you.
> *—Luke 11:9*

Discovering truth

In some of my earlier research I was intrigued by the work of Dr. Nathan Pritikin, who was considered a "radical" in the 1970s for espousing low-fat nutrition for the treatment of and therapy for heart disease, high blood pressure and diabetes.

As early as the 1920s and 1930s there had been a number of scientific articles published demonstrating that eating properly could be used to treat diabetes and even eliminate insulin therapy in some patients. Some of my physician associates are dismayed that they are often not taught these things in medical school. I am saddened to report that even today, very little nutrition is taught in our medical schools.

I have personally witnessed severely ill people who suffered from degenerative disease recover and return to vital health through diet and exercise. I have seen people use alternative health measures so successfully that they were able to throw their insulin away because they didn't need it any longer. Other patients lowered their blood pressure enough to get off medication; even angina pain disappeared for some. On the other hand, I have witnessed heart patients leave the hospital loaded up with prescriptions from their doctors, only to return in a short time for further treatment or surgery.

> **I have discovered that when the immune system is protected and strong, and when the five elimination systems of the body are functioning efficiently, the body will purely and simply correct itself, no matter what set of symptoms you are suffering that define a certain degenerative disease.**

What we gradually learned was that when we change our lifestyles by eating healthier, exercising, taking supplements and protecting ourselves from a toxic environment, we get to the root of the problem causing our illness. These alternative health measures do not simply mask the symptoms of disease as many drugs do.

My protocol does not concentrate on one ailment, set of symptoms or correction of an organ system, which is the approach of conventional medicine to illness. The underlying philosophy of the protocol is that because all the systems of the body are interconnected, a problem with one affects the others, resulting in a lessening of the overall functioning capacity of the body. I have discovered that when the immune system is protected and strong, and when the five elimination systems of the body are functioning efficiently, the body will purely and simply correct itself, no matter what set of symptoms you are suffering that define a certain degenerative disease. The solution to health problems, then, lies in fixing the underlying system that impacts the total body—the immune system.

Your wonderful "built-in" defense system

It has been my experience that with good nutrition, a therapeutic formula of vitamins, minerals and herbs, and the right kind of exercise, health is almost always dramatically improved. Through this alternative, natural approach to health, the immune system is strengthened, and the patient typically returns to deep, restorative sleep. With a drug-free, natural approach to health, patients can more readily achieve deep sleep, which is a strong healing factor. It is in deep sleep (level 4) that critical hormones, healing endorphins and key brain neuropeptides are produced to ensure a healthy, fully functioning body.

Drugs that mask symptoms, such as Elavil, Prozac, Zoloft and other antidepressants, are not the answer to common ills. Patients do not generally wake up refreshed after having been drugged with antidepressants. Also, being drug dependent for an extended time compromises and weakens the immune system, causing the body to become more vulnerable for systemic problems and illnesses. This is a fact that our medical community must hasten to realize.

Testimonial ～

After being struck with fibromyalgia a year and a half ago, I didn't think my life would ever be the same. Early on, I struggled with terrible pain, stiffness, headaches and depression, which were overwhelming to me—I felt trapped in my own body. My life was spiraling out of control, and I didn't know where to begin my journey for recovery. Prescribed medications had helped the pain, but their side effects caused more problems. I felt that my healthcare professionals were only helping me disguise the symptoms with medications instead of treating the cause of my illness.

That was when I realized I had to be the one to find my path to recovery. I wanted real answers. I wanted some doctor or some book to tell me: If you do this, you will feel better. I wanted to fix the root of the problem and regain some sense of normalcy.

I bought a journal and began a new approach to my recovery. I started recording my thoughts and logging my days, keeping tabs on what activities I did, what foods I ate and where my pain level was each day. I was looking for a pattern, some indication from my lifestyle of what I did to make me feel better on my better days. After several weeks of doing this, I realized that on the days that I ate a healthy diet and did moderate physical activity, my pain and headaches were much better and my attitude was not so negative.

Based on that discovery, I decided I needed to eat healthier. I made arrangements with a friend to visit an organic grocery store one hour from my home. I bought a few items, and on my way to the register I stumbled on a book called *Reversing Fibromyalgia* by Dr. Joe M. Elrod. I was impressed with the title, bought the book and read it through that night—and my life has never been the same. This was the first time that I had read positive words that gave hope for recovery from fibromyalgia.

Dr. Elrod's holistic and all-natural approach made logical sense and was something I wanted to learn. As I began implementing his healing protocol, the results were amazing. I felt alive again, like I just woke up from another life. My muscles gradually began to stop aching, my headaches completely disappeared, my spirit lifted to a new high, and I had energy. I was so happy. At this point I knew I would never stop living this way—it was working.

This dramatic change took about two weeks of following Dr. Elrod's health protocol. My symptoms did get worse before they got better. Dr. Elrod warned me that this would happen, so I decided to trust what he said and stay positive. At the end of two weeks, I felt almost normal again and began to live my normal lifestyle. I began doing yard work, playing outside with my kids, taking long walks and even going for ten-mile bike rides—just like before my illness began.

I knew I had to devise a new lifestyle for myself and stick to the plan or I would be right back where I was a few months earlier. First, I started with the mind-body-spirit connection. I knew this was going to be the biggest tool for my recovery. I started educating myself on this subject and learned the importance of the mind-body connection and what effects it has on the body.

The next step I concentrated on was my diet. I knew this was going to be the most challenging area for me. My eating lifestyle would not be as "convenient" as the one that made me sick. I started by eating three balanced meals a day with plenty of fruits and vegetables and a snack in between. Dr. Elrod's book gave me plenty of information to work with, and I began charting a list of bad eating habits and chemicals I needed to avoid.

The third step was to implement an exercise program, which

seemed inconceivable at the time. My muscles were so sore already, I couldn't imagine exercise making them any better. I started out very slowly with walking and Dr. Elrod's recommended stretching exercises. The stiffness and pain did get worse for a short time; I was aware this was going to happen from not using my muscles for so long. Before long, I noticed a definite improvement in my pain level, and my strength was coming back.

Getting restful sleep was my next step, which I knew was important in the recovery of fibromyalgia patients. I began to learn meditation and deep-breathing techniques to help with relaxation. The mind-body-spiritual connection also helps bring contentment to my mind and allows for a restful sleep.

Taking supplements was about the easiest step to my recovery. I started taking the recommended supplements in Dr. Elrod's book and began making it part of my everyday routine. I have successfully changed my lifestyle, following Dr. Elrod's complete protocol, and the results have been amazing. I truly believe in this program.

—Kelly Lord
Pennsylvania

Everyone can benefit

Many people give up, losing hope because they think they have suffered too many years without finding any real relief. They feel they are too old for anything positive to be possible at this point for them. The truth is that I have seen people with heart problems, high blood pressure, diabetes, extreme obesity and even fibromyalgia improve drastically. After following my protocol, people discover that their lives are greatly improved, no matter what their age is or how long they have been sick.

I encourage you to give yourself a chance to hope again, if you are presently suffering, and to make a commitment to the protocol discussed in this book that has helped so many people regain their health. Taking responsibility for what you can do and looking to God for what He wants to do for your healing are two powerful keys to your future of health and happiness.

My desire for writing this book is to help you discover and enjoy a healthier, more abundant way of life, fulfilling God's great desire and promise to us. The Body Advantage Program I have developed is about getting the total person on track—physically, mentally, emotionally and spiritually.

I have been personally inspired by the words of the prophet Habakkuk:

> Then the LORD answered me and said, "Write the vision and make it plain on tablets, that he may run who reads it. For the vision is yet for an appointed time; but at the end it will speak, and it will not lie. Though it tarries, wait for it; because it will surely come, it will not tarry.
>
> —*Habakkuk 2:2–3*

PART I

*Courageously Addressing
Your Health Issues*

CHAPTER 1

Preparing Mentally and Emotionally for Health

Choices That Make a Difference

For as he thinks in his heart, so is he.
—Proverbs 23:7

Before behavioral changes can effectively take place, we must first change the way we think and examine our emotional status. Our mental and emotional readiness are critical factors for achieving success in any endeavor we may decide to pursue, whether it be a health program, a financial plan, a career move or educational study.

During the twenty-five years I have been helping people battle systemic illnesses, regain their health and maintain it, I have gained a bit of extremely important wisdom regarding an effective approach to healing. I have learned that one of the keys that determines the level of success of patients is the way they think—their attitudes and their mental and emotional readiness. Scripture alludes to this key to success many times, telling us how our thoughts affect us. (See Proverbs 23:7.) The Old Testament prophet understood the importance of knowledge when he declared:

> My people are destroyed for lack of knowledge.
>
> *—Hosea 4:6*

CHOOSE JOY AND CULTIVATE HOPE

Part of your emotional preparation for moving toward health is to make conscious choices regarding your thoughts and emotional outlook. Choosing to experience God's divine joy should be your initial response to your recovery plan. Joy, depression and a dampened spirit cannot coexist. In the same way that darkness and light cannot coexist, because light dispels darkness, so joy dispels depression.

Even when pain and suffering fill our lives, we must make choices to overcome them by putting our hope in God. The psalmist gave us some keen insight to this key to experiencing joy:

> Hope in God, for I shall yet praise Him for the help of His countenance.
>
> *—Psalm 42:5*

The psalmist understood that putting hope in God would result in joy that would come when God gave him the help he needed. He knew that hope changes discouragement to joy. Hope gives us vision beyond where we are; it enables us to look up to the light from our darkest corners. It is true that the darkest hour of the night is always just before the dawn. When we place our hope in the love of God, the dawn will always come. God's love (*agape*) guarantees that our healing, joy and abundance are only a "faith" step away. Jesus gives us a wonderful promise when we place our faith in Him:

> If you ask anything in My name, I will do it.
>
> *—John 14:14*

Preparing mentally and emotionally is a critical factor for your success in life. In beginning any new endeavor, whether in the area of health, finances or relationships, we very often rush in without evaluating or considering where we are mentally and emotionally. This oversight can and does frequently contribute to the failure of a worthwhile venture before we really get started.

Hope changes discouragement to joy.

Begin with a positive attitude.

As we put our trust in God, the Holy Spirit gives us the power to control all of our thoughts. The Scriptures declare:

> For God did not give us a spirit of timidity, but a spirit of power, of love and of self-discipline.
>
> —*2 Timothy 1:7, NIV*

A valid translation for *self-discipline* in this passage is "sound mind" (as in the King James Version). God gives us the power to discipline our minds so that we can think healthy thoughts; we can choose joy. The same divine power that created the stars and holds them in place is given to us to help us determine the way we think.

When we allow our minds to be preoccupied with thoughts of defeat, negativity and despair, it impedes our positive actions and sets us up for failure. These kinds of "junk" thoughts create worry and stress, which result in compromising and weakening the immune system, thus opening the door for illness and disease.

The good news is that we can plug in to the divine power source in God to keep our minds in the mode of success, good health and abundance. God's Word instructs us how to successfully do this:

> Finally, brethren, whatever is true, whatever is honorable, whatever is right, whatever is pure, whatever is lovely, whatever is of good repute, if there is any excellence and if anything worthy of praise, let your mind dwell on these things. The things you have learned and received and heard and seen in me, practice these things; and the God of peace shall be with you.
>
> —*Philippians 4:8–9, NAS*

DEPRESSION, FEAR AND TEMPTATION—MAJOR CULPRITS

Depression, fear and temptation are major obstacles that often play havoc with our goals and good intentions for our lives. When we are faced with these obstacles, we need to remember the promise of the Word of God that we are not given a spirit of timidity or fear; we are given a spirit of love, power and self-discipline. (See 2 Timothy 1:6–7.) And the Scriptures promise a way out when we are tempted:

> No temptation has overtaken you except such as is common to man; but God is faithful, who will not allow you to be tempted beyond what you are able, but with the temptation will also make the way of escape, that you may be able to bear it.
>
> —*1 Corinthians 10:13*

The wonderful hope this message gives us is that God gives us all the tools to enjoy mental and emotional stability continuously, if we choose to do so. Our only requirement is to discipline ourselves to think positively as He gives us the power to do so. We should pray continuously that the Lord shields us from distractions, including mental and emotional states that can defeat the good purposes that God intends for us to carry out in His service.

OUR UNIQUE PURPOSE

It is important to understand that God has designed a special purpose for which each one of us was placed on this earth, a kind of blueprint for our lives. We are all given special gifts, talents and tools to be developed for use in serving others. That unique purpose is written on our hearts by God, who desires for us to discover it and fulfill it as we seek Him. For many people, the lack of understanding purpose causes them to despair and become depressed. They are not aware of the wonderful promise that declares:

> **When we get in touch with our purpose, we can discover who we are and why we are here on this earth. Then we begin to experience a fullness of joy and a peace that is almost incomprehensible.**

> For we are His workmanship, created in Christ Jesus for good works, which God prepared beforehand that we should walk in them.
>
> —*Ephesians 2:10*

When we choose to put our faith in Christ and get in touch with our purpose, we can discover who we are and why we are here on this earth. Then we begin to experience a fullness of joy and a peace that is almost incomprehensible. I firmly believe this is why God instructs us to ask, to seek and to knock:

> Ask, and it will be given to you; seek, and you will find; knock, and it will be opened to you. For everyone who asks receives, and he who seeks finds, and to him who knocks it will be opened. Or what man is there among you who, if his son asks for bread, will give him a stone? Or if he asks for a fish, will he give him a serpent? If you then,

being evil, know how to give good gifts to your children, how much more will your Father who is in heaven give good things to those who ask Him!

—Matthew 7:7–12

Jesus promises very clearly that if we ask, He will answer us; if we seek, we will find; and if we knock, it will be opened unto us. Discovering God's purpose for our lives is a key to establishing our thoughts and emotions in health. Understanding the goodness of God and believing His promises to us will change our entire outlook on life. The Scriptures declare that to enjoy His promises and walk in His purposes we have only to seek Him:

"For I know the plans that I have for you," declares the LORD, "plans for welfare and not for calamity to give you a future and a hope. Then you will call upon Me and come and pray to Me, and I will listen to you. And you will seek Me and find Me."

—Jeremiah 29:11–13, NAS

Call to Me, and I will answer you, and I will tell you great and mighty things.

—Jeremiah 33:3, NAS

The conditions attached to these wonderful promises that God lays out for us are not difficult. He offers free gifts and blessings, but we have to receive them in faith and move forward to accomplish our purpose; God will not do that for us. Do you remember when God was speaking to Moses about his appointment to be a deliverer of God's people and a spokesman for them?

Moses balked and told God that he was not capable of leading or speaking. God assured Moses that He would be with him and provide what was needed to establish his purpose and fulfill his mission. God was requiring that Moses trust Him and move out in faith to accomplish this great task. (See Exodus 4.)

The writer of Proverbs knew how important it is to depend on the Lord when he wrote:

Commit your works to the LORD, and your plans will be established.

—Proverbs 16:3, NAS

SUPERIOR SOURCE FOR SPIRITUAL HEALTH

One of the most effective ways to gain and maintain mental and emotional health is to read the Bible, God's Word, for instruction, inspiration and direction for your life. If you have not practiced the study of His Word, you will be absolutely amazed when you begin to read the Bible and see how God will reveal your blueprint for life, piece by piece, in His timing and as you are ready for it. I have learned that God's timing is always perfect.

For you who are attempting to recover from systemic conditions and degenerative disease, the Bible is filled with verses that refer to God's promises for healing that will build your faith to receive it. The following are verses that would be helpful while beginning your recovery and healing process:

> Bless the LORD, O my soul,
> And forget not all His benefits:
> Who forgives all your iniquities,
> Who heals all your diseases,
> Who redeems your life from destruction,
> Who crowns you with lovingkindness and tender mercies,
> Who satisfies your mouth with good things,
> So that your youth is renewed like the eagle's.
>
> —*Psalm 103:2–3*

> I will give thanks to Thee, for I am fearfully and wonderfully made;
> Wonderful are Thy works,
> And my soul knows it very well.
>
> —*Psalm 139:14, NAS*

Systemic illness and degenerative disease are often challenges of life we face as a result of bad decisions and our abusive lifestyles. God has never promised to eliminate the challenges or control our lifestyle decisions. We are responsible to be stewards of the life He gives to us—physically, mentally and spiritually. What He has promised is that He will never leave us or forsake us. (See Hebrews 13:5.) The Scriptures teach us that He is our healer, our protector, our provider and the source of our strength. The psalmist gives us a beautiful picture of these characteristics of our awesome Creator:

I will lift up my eyes to the hills—
From whence comes my help?
My help comes from the LORD,
Who made heaven and earth.

He will not allow your foot to be moved;
He who keeps you will not slumber.
Behold, He who keeps Israel
Shall neither slumber nor sleep.

The LORD is your keeper;
The LORD is your shade at your right hand.
The sun shall not strike you by day,
Nor the moon by night.

The LORD shall preserve you from all evil;
He shall preserve your soul.
The LORD shall preserve your going out and your
    coming in
From this time forth, and even forevermore.

—Psalm 121

Hope for a nation at risk

As a nation, we are self-destructing in the area of our health. We are subjecting ourselves to a multitude of environmental toxins; we are creating appetites for and consuming all the wrong kinds of foods; we are consistently experiencing chronic fatigue because of our "fast-lane" lifestyles—and yet we wonder why we are battling degenerative disease. As a scientific researcher and medical author, it troubles me deeply to see so many people of all ages struggling with chronic and degenerative disease that can be easily reversed and eliminated.

My good friend, on the following pages I will share with you how you can live in vibrant health and enjoy strength, energy and a better quality of life all of your days. Though it is sometimes challenging to make technical information simple and understandable, in writing this book it has been my mission to reach you with a workable plan. My mission has been to provide in these pages a workable, healing protocol based on biblical principles.

I strongly believe that God has the power to heal, and that, according to 3 John 2, He desires for His people to live in health and prosper. I have personally witnessed many miracles of healing through the power of God and wise choices for healthy lifestyles to which people commit.

It is my prayer that the material in this book will provide you with the knowledge you need to regain and maintain divine health. I trust that you will also discover more perfectly your unique purpose for which God created you and learn to enjoy the delight of fulfilling that God-given purpose in serving others.

CHAPTER 2

How to Be Healthy for Life

Introducing The Body Advantage Program

> I will praise You, for I am fearfully and wonderfully made; marvelous are Your works, and that my soul knows very well.
>
> —PSALM 139:14

Living a healthy, productive life with peace of mind and heart is everyone's dream. We hear the term *wellness* used frequently when referring to fitness for the total person, including mental, physical, emotional and spiritual components. This includes being physically fit and strong, maintaining a healthy weight and feeling emotionally secure with a positive self-image. For many, this is a dream that is too good to be true. Learning to make right decisions and choosing to accept the challenge of change will bring us to a higher level of healing and health—total wellness—that God desires to give to us.

As we consider the wonderful fact of our existence and begin to understand the purpose of the Creator for our lives, we can dream the dream for total wellness and begin to achieve positive results. The psalmist was keenly aware of the phenomenal creative work involved in a human being when he considered the wonder of his being. (See Psalm 139:14.)

TOTAL WELLNESS DEFINED

Total fitness or wellness involves much broader concepts than many people realize. It includes the areas of basic fitness, musculoskeletal fitness, cardiovascular fitness and mental or emotional fitness. A brief discussion of each of these areas of wellness will help us to get started toward our personal goals for health. It will also introduce you to the three phases of The Body Advantage Program. (See Part IV for details.)

Basic fitness

Basic fitness generally refers to your ability to perform the routine tasks of daily life safely and efficiently. It would support those movements necessary on a daily basis, such as walking, bending, lifting and climbing stairs. Phase I of this program will prepare you through basic, low-impact exercises for success in Phase II and Phase III of the program, as well as for life. These basic exercises will safely increase your muscular strength, flexibility (stretch-ability), balance and coordination. They will also increase the strength and endurance of your abdominal muscles, your back and the stabilizing muscles of your shoulders and lower legs for bending and lifting.

Musculoskeletal fitness

Musculoskeletal fitness includes the muscles, ligaments and tendons of the total body musculature and the connective tissues encompassing muscular strength, flexibility and endurance. These fitness objectives are accomplished through the use of weights (in Phases II and III) and/or the use of The Body Advantage exercise device, which may be used in all phases of the program. (See the chapter eight and the product page for more information on The Body Advantage Exercise System.)

Cardiovascular fitness

Cardiovascular fitness relates to the health of your heart, lungs and blood vessels. Their fitness is improved and maintained primarily through aerobic exercises. Aerobic exercises are those that cause exertion for the heart, lungs and legs, such as walking, jogging, mountain biking, stationary cycling and aerobic classes. Cardiovascular exercise is an important step in all three phases of The Body Advantage Program.

Mental and emotional fitness

Total wellness must include the important areas of mental and emotional fitness, as we have discussed. Being loved, having an opportunity to love and feeling a healthy sense of self-worth are important factors that contribute much to your physical health. Feeling that you are contributing to your fellow man, feeling protected, enjoying financial security, receiving appreciation and experiencing companionship are all basic human needs that we desperately seek to fulfill. It is important to become aware of your mental and emotional health and to understand how these vital areas affect your physical health.

When any of our basic human needs are missing from our lives, our feeling of lack can lead to stress, boredom, loneliness and even depression. When added to poor diet and nutritional deficiencies, lack of exercise, and accumulation of toxins from refined foods, air and water, the result is a weakened immune system and a lowered level of natural killer (NK) cells.

Traumatic emotional and/or physical experiences such as toxic relationships, divorce, auto accidents, bankruptcy, a distasteful job or the loss of a loved one tend to exacerbate underlying conditions and accelerate the down-spiraling effect of a damaged immune system, which leads eventually to illness. When several of these "life situations" happen concurrently, an individual can become unbalanced hormonally and nutritionally and begin to exhibit poor health characteristics, such as a disrupted sleep pattern.

When a person becomes toxic at the cellular level, he or she loses the ability to reach level 4 sleep (the deep, restorative sleep cycle). Without proper rest, the body cannot refurbish, ward off fatigue or produce hormones efficiently. Rest is also a major prerequisite for systemic balance that enables the body to remain healthy and efficient for daily biological functions.

The Body Advantage Program is designed to assist you in reversing the unhealthy state I have described by strengthening your immune system, achieving your best weight, stopping the degenerative disease process and restoring you to the maximal state of health that is possible for you. You deserve the very best that life has to offer, and that includes a vibrant, abundant, healthy and productive pain-free lifestyle.

GETTING ON TRACK FOR THE TOTAL YOU!

The Body Advantage Program I have designed is a protocol for doing the right things, the scientifically proven things that work on a permanent basis to ensure healthful living. It is a program that will help you make choices to do the right things for health, making necessary lifestyle changes realistically and gradually.

This program will not only guide you to more intelligent healthy choices about nourishing and strengthening your body, nurturing your emotional well-being and self-worth, and moving through challenges that you haven't been able to conquer in the past; it will also help you change the way you think. The first goal of my program is to assist you in learning to overcome emotional and psychological challenges in order to keep you on track for success.

In summary, this is a program for life—for anyone and everyone—for people of every size, shape, weight, age and gender. This program for health has already guided many people into a simple, easy-to-follow progression of a healthful lifestyle.

PROGRAM GOALS

The total program I have designed allows you to move at your own pace while assisting you to accomplish the goals of preventing or reversing degenerative disease and establishing a toned, healthier body to enjoy a productive, active lifestyle. By carefully following this simple program, you can expect help in:

- Assisting you to lose and/or maintain weight effectively and healthfully

- Correcting an illness or systemic condition that you may be challenged with currently

- Building a strong immune system that will assist you now and in the future

- Establishing an emotional balance to get in touch with healthier relationships and to better control emotional eating triggers

- Enjoying a more positive self-image and feeling good about yourself

- Adjusting thought patterns to help create positive change

In order to move toward more healthy living, as we have said, you must take responsibility for your choices that affect your health. As you do, you will fulfill your part to receive the promise of God for your health:

> Give attention to my words; incline your ear to my sayings. Do not let them depart from your sight; keep them in the midst of your heart. For they are life to those who find them, and health to all their whole body.
>
> —*Proverbs 4:20–22,* NAS

OBTAINING MEDICAL CLEARANCE

Always consult your physician before you begin a wellness program. Have your physician complete the chart on page 33 before starting this Body Advantage Program.

COMMITMENT DEFINED

Commitment is what transforms a promise into reality. It is the words that speak boldly of our intentions and the actions that speak louder than the words. It is making the time when there is none—coming through time after time after time, year after year. Commitment is the material of which character is made, the power to change the face of things. It is the daily triumph of integrity over skepticism.

THE CHALLENGE OF CHANGE

Have you ever begun a health program with the intent of losing weight, getting your energy back, healing your body or getting rid of pain? Did you ever start a program and lose your motivation or quit simply because it wasn't working? If this has happened to you, there's a good chance that you were not ready mentally and emotionally for such challenging changes. The instructions of the previous chapter regarding this preparation are not optional; they are strategic to your success.

Another key factor to your previous lack of success may be that your immune system needed some strengthening and preparation in order for you to have been successful in reaching an optimal level of fitness.

You cannot lose weight efficiently, get your energy back, heal your body, get rid of pain or restore a healthy sleep pattern until you are mentally and emotionally ready. Then, you need to position yourself to be successful in achieving your goals for optimal health through cleansing and detoxifying, returning to restful sleep, starting a sound nutritional program, using nutritional supplements, exercising and reducing stress. This program will guide you successfully to do exactly that.

Tips for success

In this chapter, I want to introduce you to the concepts of my twelve-week program, which will be discussed in-depth in the following chapters. I want to help you assimilate those concepts and begin to believe that this program will work for you. Here are some tips that will help you begin:

- Make a firm commitment to change.

- Identify and write down the reasons you want to change.

- Write down your goals for the next three months.

- Identify and write down three patterns of behavior that have held you back from change.

- Identify and write down three new positive patterns of behavior that will help you succeed.

- Begin working on replacing the old habit patterns with the new ones by keeping a daily log.

- Review what you have written every morning for twelve weeks. Revise and edit your written goals and your daily log each Friday. Keep a calendar.

This part of the program is designed to make you think, to identify bad habits or emotional hang-ups, and to help you develop healthy thought patterns. (The following form and worksheet are for the above activities. Note: A workbook guide is also available for the twelve-week program. Please see the product page to order.)

ATTITUDE ASSESSMENT QUESTIONNAIRE

Check *Yes* or *No* for each question. Make notes as you think about your answer and the healthy adjustments you would like to make for each.

Yes No

Do you become impatient or inconsistent when progress is slow? ☐ ☐

Adjustments needed: _____

_____

Yes No

Is procrastinating ever a problem? ☐ ☐

Adjustments needed: _____

_____

Yes No

Do you fear or resist change? ☐ ☐

Adjustments needed: _____

_____

Yes No

Do you ever make excuses to get around what is necessary to reach your goals? ☐ ☐

Adjustments needed: _____

_____

	Yes	No
Do you think that you will be happy and content once you achieve a particular size or weight, get your energy back or get healthier?	☐	☐

Adjustments needed:

_____

_____

	Yes	No
Are you afraid of what others think, and are you concerned about disappointing them?	☐	☐

Adjustments needed:

_____

_____

	Yes	No
Do you sometimes feel that you don't deserve to be happy or successful?	☐	☐

Adjustments needed:

_____

_____

	Yes	No
Have you ever used career, family or relationships as an excuse not to take care of yourself?	☐	☐

Adjustments needed:

_____

_____

	Yes	No
When you have flare-ups or setbacks, do you ever consider quitting or giving up?	☐	☐

Adjustments needed:

_____

_____

If you have honestly assessed your attitudes and identified adjustments you need to make to succeed in your quest for health, you are already on your way to restoration. You are ready to make a commitment to change unhealthy patterns in your life so that you can enjoy the health you were created to enjoy. I challenge you to take your next step toward wholeness by filling out the worksheet on page 32.

MY PLAN FOR SUCCESS WORKSHEET

My commitment to change:

I, _____, here and now make a commitment to change.

Three reasons I want to change:

1.

2.

3.

My goals for the next three months:

1. Physical:

2. Mental/emotional:

3. Family/relationships:

Behavioral patterns I need to change:

1.

2.

3.

New behavioral patterns I want to begin:

1.

2.

3.

To help you succeed:

• Keep a daily log.

• Review these goals regularly and make adjustments as needed.

PERSONAL MEDICAL DATA

Compare these measurements after twelve weeks to evaluate your progress. These data are critical to your health over the long term.

Your Data	Beginning	After 12 Weeks
Weight		
Blood pressure		
Total cholesterol		
HDL cholesterol		
LDL cholesterol		
Total/HDL cholesterol ratio		
Blood sugar		

CHAPTER 3

Six Natural Steps to Total Wellness

A Simple Model for Health

**Beloved, I pray that you may prosper in all things
and be in health, just as your soul prospers.**
—3 John 2

The graphic on the next page represents the six steps of The Body Advantage Program that, when present, represent total wellness. All six factors are necessary to return to and maintain a vibrant, healthful lifestyle. Each factor complements the other, working synergistically to complete your perfect health plan and to restore you to total wellness.

My twelve-week program is designed to help you succeed by establishing these six factors as optimal goals for health. I will show you how to change your unhealthy thought patterns psychologically and replace them with patterns that lead to stress relief, wellness and success. The program helps to resolve trauma, pain and inflammation by lowering the impact of damaging toxins and free radicals and by stimulating the building and healing process. Shopping for and preparing food is simple, and the exercise is low impact, stimulating and fun.

A SIMPLE MODEL FOR HEALTH:
SIX KEY FACTORS

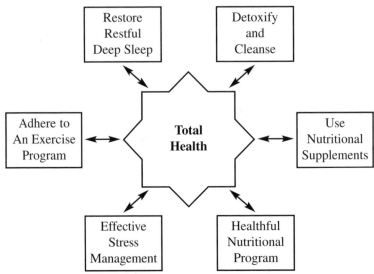

ONE PROGRAM—THREE PHASES

The Body Advantage Program I have developed involves three well-defined phases that I refer to as balancing, progressing and maintaining facets of your total wellness plan. As your goals for health continue to increase, you will pass through these three phases again, maintaining former goals while progressing to new ones. You can evaluate your progress by understanding the basic definition of each phase. (See Part IV for detailed protocol.)

It is critically important for you to understand that this is not a "fad regimen" that ends once you achieve your goals, allowing you to return to the old lifestyle that made you become unhealthy. This program is the beginning of a lifestyle that you will pursue for life so that you can enjoy health, joy and abundance.

Phase I: Balancing

Phase I is about commitment and preparation for change. This phase involves mental, emotional and physical preparation. If we fail to make a firm mental commitment before making a change, we will not succeed in the change we desire. Normally we resist change. However, change is inevitable, and the sooner we develop positive attitudes about change, the sooner we will move on in positive directions. This commitment to and acceptance of change will multiply our success ratio exponentially.

This program will help you to work on making simple changes for your body. More importantly, it will assist you in determining the proper mind-set that will serve as the key to your success. I will show you how to set some of your personal goals and coach you in writing them. If you have never written them down, you will find it an extremely powerful exercise. You will also have an opportunity to perform some written exercises that will help you get in touch with personal issues regarding your self-image, your attitudes, your health, your happiness and any potentially self-destructive habits.

Simply put, you will get in touch with your inner feelings about unconscious attitudes toward making changes in your life. You will also discover why success has escaped you in particular areas in the past.

Phase II: Progressing

Phase II involves progressing toward your ultimate goals in the major areas of life. Having initiated the changes of Phase I, you will have begun to make progress with attitudes and emotions as well as enjoying greater strength, more energy and clear thinking. You will also begin to experience definite changes in your body, the way your clothes fit and the positive thoughts you have about yourself.

Phase III: Maintaining

Phase III involves maintaining once you have accomplished some significant goals that established improved personal routines as a lifestyle. Once you have reached your first goals, this protocol will serve you as you set new, exciting goals in other areas with the potential of greater success in personal, family and financial areas. Remember, there may be setbacks, but with persistence, determination and a committed effort—you will succeed.

MODEL FOR REVERSING DEGENERATIVE DISEASE

Step 1—De-stress your life: Balancing and setting the stage

Step 2—Detoxify your body: Discovering a key to good health

Step 3—Eat for life: Adding years and quality of life

Step 4—Supplement for efficiency: Enhancing energy

Step 5—Become active: Unlocking the power of exercise

Step 6—Restore deep sleep: Refurbishing and healing the mind and body

THE BODY'S HEALING POTENTIAL

Are you aware of how critical nutrition and natural supplements are to the health and wellness process? Do you know that every six to eight years your total body (bones, organs, skin, every cell) has been made anew, or re-created? As you are reading this, old cells are degenerating and dying as new cells are being regenerated to replace them.

Isn't this an exciting fact? No matter what the autoimmune problem, disease or systemic condition, by gaining the knowledge and doing the right things consistently, you can get better, have more energy, get rid of pain and return to health and vitality. This is possible because of the body's ability to regenerate or re-create itself through developing new cells—building blocks for healthy tissue and bone.

> **"Let your food be your medicine, let your medicine be your food."**
>
> **—Hippocrates**

For example, fibromyalgia sufferers are being told worldwide that they cannot get well—that's pure hogwash. Consider the devastating muscle pain. If we are re-creating new muscle fiber every six to eight months, wouldn't it be logical to expect that when we change eating habits, exercise habits and other lifestyle patterns, we can regenerate strong, healthy, pain-free muscle fiber? The answer is emphatically *yes*, we absolutely can.

And the wonderful news is that it doesn't have to be complicated. One of my joys as a teacher is to share with you these healing principles so simply that it's easy reading, user friendly and failure proof. If you follow every step of my program, you will succeed.

THE BODY ADVANTAGE WELLNESS CONTRACT

Acknowledging that only I can define the word *success* for myself, I, _____,
agree that my success plan can be designed only by me and fulfilled by my consistent, determined actions. I agree that commitment to my plan is the first step in achieving the success that I desire. I will use this plan to set my goals, and I will use this plan to track my success.

I recognize that to reach my goals and to realize my fullest potential, I must strive consistently with a positive mental attitude. I promise to work daily at improving my skills and increasing my knowledge to achieve the realization of becoming all that I was intended to be. Finally, I will commit to following this plan.

_____*Signature*

_____*Date*

Part II

Implementing the Vital Steps to Health

CHAPTER 4

Step 1: De-stress Your Life

Balancing and Setting the Stage

A joyful heart is good medicine.
—PROVERBS 17:22, NAS

I believe these times are more stressful than any other in the history of mankind. In today's fast-paced world, we face extreme pressures in the workplace, with our finances, in personal relationships and with our uncertainty concerning world conflict and insecurity. If you are feeling overwhelmed and are looking for relief and answers, you can expect to find both in these pages.

You can conquer stress with its devastating effects. There is hope for you—as you decide to take control of your life and destiny through faith, prayer and confidence. Jesus promised His disciples that, although He was leaving them to return to His Father, He would give them a gift—peace of mind and heart. He declared:

> Peace I leave with you, My peace I give to you; not as the world gives do I give to you. Let not your heart be troubled, neither let it be afraid.
>
> *—John 14:27*

STRESS: THE HEALTH THIEF

As a Christian medical author and researcher, I have studied and prayed about the debilitating effects of degenerative disease. Without exception, patients with whom I have had the privilege of working have always experienced emotional and spiritual upheaval. Thus, I have concluded that most degenerative disease and systemic conditions have a spiritual basis. If you have read my books and followed my research, you are aware that I firmly believe in a close link between body, mind and spirit. They are intricately connected and cannot be separated as traditional medicine and practices often try to do. Many of the distresses we suffer in the body have their beginnings in our minds, emotions and spirits. Stress is one of the major culprits that rob us of our health. The impact of stress is simply devastating to the body. Many sources support the fact that stress is a primary force for encouraging cancer cells in the body as well as other degenerative diseases such as arthritis, lupus, Crohn's disease, psoriasis and fibromyalgia.

Many people who overeat as a result of stress are trying to use food to help them cope with the trials and tribulations of life. Their addiction to food, while giving perhaps momentary comfort, creates serious health problems, similar to what happens with other kinds of addictions. Overeating is not a true antidote for stress; it further stresses the body, thus causing it to be toxic, which leads to a cycle of poor health. The peace sought by those who overeat eludes them because they are looking for it in the wrong places.

One answer to stress is spiritual.

Food cannot provide true peace. True peace comes through a close relationship with our Creator, whose Holy Spirit gives us peace from within. As much as we try to delude ourselves that something else can comfort us, the fact is that true peace cannot be found in external sources of material objects or even in relationships with people.

When we seek God through His living Word and through prayer, He fills us with His peace and joy. Scripture tells us that if we keep our minds focused on the right things and walk in faith and love, God will fill us with His perfect peace. The prophet Isaiah understood this wonderful promise when he wrote:

> The steadfast of mind Thou wilt keep in perfect peace,
> because he trusts in Thee.
>
> —Isaiah 26:3, NAS

Once again we see the importance of the body-mind connection as it relates to stress and our health. Though there are natural things we can do and ways we can eat to reduce the effects of stress, we cannot eliminate the important part our minds play in our reaction to life's events. Changing our attitudes of worry and despair to enthusiasm and even-mindedness has a powerful healing effect on our bodies. There are pervasive anatomic and biochemical links between the immune and nervous systems that help explain the influence of mood on our susceptibility to disease. Scripture teaches us that it is possible to change our negative thinking patterns. Listen to the apostle Paul's concerned instructions:

> I beseech you therefore, brethren, by the mercies of God, that you present your bodies a living sacrifice, holy, acceptable to God, which is your reasonable service. And do not be conformed to this world, but be transformed by the renewing of your mind, that you may prove what is that good and acceptable and perfect will of God.
>
> —*Romans 12:1–2*

Renewing our minds with the wonderful promises of the Word of God will help us to find His will for our lives, an important part of which is the health He desires for us. As we surrender our lives to God and allow His Word to fill our minds and hearts with peace and hope, we will find our stress levels diminishing, and the will of God for our health will become a reality.

A recent survey revealed that more than 50 percent of health problems are related to the effects of stress. It also concluded that an overwhelming percentage of workplace problems are stress related.[1] Let me encourage you that you can be victorious over stress. Begin to tap into the power of God; walk in faith and believe that you can have the peace He offers—peace that rises above the troubles of this world.

As we learn to be filled with His Spirit, we can enjoy the wonderful benefits of the abundant life He promises us. (See John 10:10.) Scripture declares:

> But the fruit of the Spirit is love, joy, peace, patience, kindness, goodness, faithfulness, gentleness, self-control; against such things there is no law.
>
> —*Galatians 5:22–23, NAS*

If you do not feel or know that you are filled with the Holy Spirit and truly want to be, then pray this simple prayer in faith:

Lord, come into my heart and fill me with Your Holy Spirit. Guide me—I truly want to know my purpose in this life. I desire to be Spirit-filled and Spirit-led. I want to serve You and serve others. I want to experience the love, joy and peace promised in Your Word. Amen.

My prayer and heart's desire is that this book will assist you in discovering God's divine plan for your health through alternative methods along with the awesome power of prayer and the Scriptures. The verses of Scripture we are including here will help you to focus on your goals and become aware of God's power to help you. You will be amazed at how it will all promote your health and assist you in better understanding God's plan for your life—a divine plan that includes overcoming stress and leads to health, happiness and fulfillment in your life.

The fact that you have this book in your hand is evidence of your seeking and finding the help you need. One of God's wonderful promises for you declares this: "Ask, and it shall be given to you; seek, and you shall find; knock, and it shall be opened to you" (Luke 11:9). The answers you need for health cannot be found in the use of chemical drugs such as Elavil, Prozac and Zoloft.

You can regain your health and well-being by choosing to address the underlying issues for which these drugs simply cover up the symptoms. Experience has proven that you can become well by utilizing the protocol in my twelve-week Body Advantage Program. As you choose to take charge of your lifestyle and seek God's help, you will follow the apostle Paul's instruction:

> And do not be conformed to this world, but be transformed by the renewing of your mind, that you may prove what is that good and acceptable and perfect will of God.
>
> *—Romans 12:2*

KEY TO SUCCESSFUL STRESS MANAGEMENT

Since stress can lead to the onset of other conditions and diseases, including depression, it is important to have the tools that we can use to overcome its negative effects. Often these tools are very simple positive steps that we can take, such as developing the positive habit of awaking each day with a thankful heart and cultivating an optimistic attitude.

These first thoughts and aspirations will go with you throughout the day. Your thoughts and emotional responses are triggering the release of endorphins and catecholamines, the healing and uplifting hormones within your immune system. By focusing on all that is hopeful, joyful, pleasant, loving and optimistic, you can take the edge off stress and continually improve your unhealthy condition as you consistently move toward a healthy existence.

Scripture supports this mental approach to health in many passages. For example, the apostle Paul exhorted us:

> Whatever things are true, whatever things are noble, whatever things are just, whatever things are pure, whatever things are lovely, whatever things are of good report, if there is any virtue and if there is anything praiseworthy—meditate on these things.
>
> *—Philippians 4:8*

TOOLS FOR DECREASING PERSONAL STRESS

We will be discussing these simple tools you can use to begin to decrease your personal stress levels. It is not difficult to use these tools, but it will be necessary for you to make a commitment to incorporate into your lifestyle the changes that are needed. In this section we will take a closer look at some of these practical stress-busting tools.

- *Boost your nutrition.* Eat more frequently, five to six times a day. Eat a balanced diet, choosing from the power foods listed in this book. Be sure that only 20 percent of your total daily diet contains fat. Avoid sugar, alcohol, tobacco and caffeine.

- *Use natural nutrients.* Be sure to read carefully chapter seven on the importance of adding supplements to your diet. If you are dealing with one of the degenerative diseases discussed in chapter ten, follow the supplement guidelines I have given for that disease or condition. Using vitamin and mineral supplements with antioxidant qualities will boost your immune system and help your body to maintain—and increase—cellular energy, cardiovascular awareness and youthful vitality.

- *Be sure to exercise.* Put into action the exercise program outlined in chapter eight. Complete some form of aerobic exercise, such as cycling, walking or swimming, at least four to five times per week. On the days that you are not exercising aerobically, complete stretching and muscle-toning exercises. Joint stretching and muscle-toning exercises will be very beneficial. Exercising regularly will increase the potential for you to move into deep sleep while resting.

- *Understand the stress-rest link.* Rest and relaxation will help you to overcome stress, and they will help to reduce muscle tension and pain. Learning the art of relaxation is most important to stress management. Get adequate amounts of sleep, focus on the positive, and visualize your goals. Avoid antidepressants and sleeping medications. Even though they may help you to get to sleep, they will suppress deep sleep and could make your symptoms worse.

- *Eliminate stress from your life.* Don't overextend yourself, and always plan ahead for difficult tasks. Ask for help whenever you need it. Prioritize your responsibilities and activities to manageable levels. Budget your time, and be realistic about your limitations.

ACTIVITIES FOR REDUCING STRESS

The following are some proven stress-reducing activities:

- Gentle stretching
- A warm bath
- A brief nap
- A walk in the woods
- Ocean or nature sounds

- Relaxing music
- Doing a favor for a friend
- Using humor frequently
- Meditation and prayer
- Mental relaxation
- Using a foot massager
- Breathing and muscle relaxation

By utilizing several of these stress-busting tools on a regular basis, you will find your stress levels decreasing, which will make it easier to include more of these relaxing activities into your daily life. This healthy cycle will increase and help you attain your goals for optimal health.

STRESS-REST LINK

Rest is vital for overcoming stress. In general, adults require between six and eight hours of sleep a night. You should determine whether you require six, seven or eight hours through experimentation and monitoring your sleep over a prolonged period. Try the following for improved rest:

- Exercise regularly, but not too close to bedtime.

- Avoid eating and ingesting stimulants after 6:00 P.M.

- Keep your bedroom quiet and dark.

- Establish a pre-sleep "unwinding" routine (for example, reading, meditating and praying).

- Refrain from taking sleeping pills.

- Organize your concerns of life and develop action plans with objectivity rather than worry.

- Always plan your day in the afternoon or evening of the day before—not the morning of that day.

RECOGNIZE THE SYMPTOMS OF DEPRESSION

Depression is a common outcome of prolonged stress, and it is important to be aware of the signs and symptoms, know how to recognize them and learn what to do to alleviate them.

There are three general levels of depression. It often begins as a one-time occurrence, lasting as little as a day or as much as several weeks. But once it leaves it does not return. The second level of depression is a recurrent depressive disorder, which appears and disappears periodically. An individual can feel very good and normal between the episodes of depression. A final level involves a chronic depressive disorder that lasts for several years, maybe even for half a lifetime or more. The symptoms on this level can be very severe in the first two to four years.

Identifying depression

If you experience symptoms of depression that do not go away or that worsen with time, you should contact your physician and/or psychologist right away. These symptoms could include:

- Irritability or blue moods
- Restlessness or a slowed-down feeling
- Appetite changes leading to weight gain or loss
- Problems with concentration, thinking or memory
- Difficulty making decisions
- Loss of interest in the things you normally enjoy
- Lack of sleep or sleeping too much
- Nightmares, especially with themes of loss, pain or death
- Constant lack of energy
- Feelings of hopelessness
- Anxiety
- Preoccupation with failure, illness, etc.
- Fear of being alone
- Feelings of worthlessness or guilt
- Low self-esteem
- Suicidal thoughts or thoughts of dying
- Lack of interest in sex
- Headaches not caused by any other disease or condition
- Other aches and pains not caused by any other condition
- Digestive problems unrelated to any other condition

TAKE A NUTRITIONAL APPROACH TO ALLEVIATE DEPRESSION

Many of the nutritional tools that you can use to alleviate stress can also be used to alleviate mild or occasional bouts with depression. If you struggle with depression, you may find it necessary to make some lifestyle changes to deal positively with your depression. Look over the following list, and check the things in the list that you need to change because they may be contributing to your depressed condition:

☐ Do you skip meals, especially breakfast?

☐ Do you consume a high quantity of sugar and highly refined foods?

☐ Does your daily fat intake exceed 20 percent of your total calories?

☐ Are you getting enough fiber in your diet? Have you increased the amount of fiber in the form of fruits, vegetables, breads, cereals and legumes? (Do this gradually so as to avoid bloating.)

☐ Are you eating a balanced diet of 40 to 60 percent carbohydrates, 15 to 20 percent fats and 10 to 20 percent protein on a daily basis?

☐ Are you maintaining an appropriate weight level?

☐ Are you limiting your intake of red meat, caffeine and alcohol?

☐ Are you still using substitute sugar substances such as NutraSweet in your diet?

☐ Are you adding healthy supplements to your diet, including antioxidants? (Suggested daily minimums are 1,000 milligrams of vitamin C, 800 International Units of vitamin E, 25,000 International Units of beta carotene, 50 milligrams of coenzyme Q_{10} and 100 milligrams per 50 pounds of body weight of pycnogenol (proanthocyanidins).

☐ Are you drinking at least 72 ounces of purified

water daily? (Water in tea and other drinks does not count toward your daily water requirement.)

Degenerative disease can produce a host of psychological changes due to anxiety, frustration, pain, depression and stress. The Body Advantage Program will assist you in healthfully managing stress and avoiding depression in several ways. By utilizing your total reversing degenerative disease program of nutrition, exercise and suggested supplements, along with stress management methods and techniques, you can be victorious in overcoming stress and depression.

STRESS—BE GONE!

In this chapter you have learned important stress-busting tools that you can use to eliminate some of the unnecessary stress from your life. These tools will also help you to overcome the depression that often is the result of too much stress. As you continue to learn about the remaining five steps of the six steps to health in the remaining chapters of this book, continue using these tools. Try these additional tools to combat stress. Stress is a necessary part of everyone's life, but you do not need to impact your quality of life because of your response to the stress in your life. Try these tools:

- Reduce caffeine and alcohol intake.
- Take hot relaxing baths.
- Try aromatherapy.
- Enjoy soft music and candlelight.
- Plan vacations and "getaways" regularly.
- Read and listen to motivational materials.
- Improve communication skills.
- Write in a journal.
- Review positive affirmations.
- Plan recreation with friends and loved ones.
- Laugh.
- Take up a hobby.
- Write and review your goals regularly.

CHAPTER 5

Step 2: Detoxify Your Body

A Key to Good Health

> Do not be wise in your own eyes; fear the LORD
> and depart from evil. It will be health to your
> flesh, and strength to your bones.
> —PROVERBS 3:7–8

We live in an extremely toxic environment in an industrialized, "chemicalized" nation. We are constantly exposed to harmful toxins from the air we breathe, the water we drink, cosmetics and household supplies, as well as the vast availability of processed and refined foods. We also experience direct exposure to heavy metals, radiation, sprays, powerful antibiotics and other drugs. Along with these outside influences on our health, we are also vulnerable to the action of free radicals from the metabolic process of our own body.

Before discussing my simple detoxification program, it will help you to become more aware of the toxic environmental hazards that contribute to your need to detoxify.

ADDITIVES, METALS AND OTHER TOXINS

Toxic metals are clearly linked to degenerative disease, along with food additives and other pollutants. Commonly found in commercially processed foods that typically contain colorings and additives, the threat of toxic metals to our health is a reality. Other pollutants that regularly contaminate our foods include agricultural chemicals and pesticides. As we discuss briefly this problem with pollutants that contaminate our foods and compromise our immune system, consider how you can avoid as many of them as you can. For more complete information on this topic, I recommend Dr. Skye Weintraub's *Natural Treatments for ADD and Hyperactivity.*[1]

METALS

Below is a list of metals commonly found in the body. If they reach toxic levels, they can cause serious degenerative health problems.

Aluminum

High levels of aluminum negatively impact the body's central nervous system. Research is available showing that aluminum may be involved in the problems of fibromyalgia and Alzheimer's disease. Amazingly, the highly advertised antacids, which Americans consume as a source of calcium, are a source of aluminum. Aluminum cookware and aluminum foil, frequently used to store food, are primary sources of this metal in the diet. It is also found in bleached flour and coffee. The toxic effects of aluminum increase greatly if deficiencies of magnesium and calcium exist in the body.

Cadmium

People who eat excessive amounts of carbohydrates—often present in fast food menus and in refined foods—usually have higher levels of cadmium. Once cadmium is in the body, it is very difficult to remove because it has a life span of seventeen to thirty years. Nutritional therapy is often necessary to eliminate cadmium from the body. Cigarettes are a major source of cadmium in our society, and galvanized iron, sometimes used for drain pipes, can contain up to 2 percent cadmium, often contaminating our tap water.

Copper

When the adrenal glands function properly, they produce a copper-bonding protein that rids the body of copper. However, stress can lead to copper toxicity by depleting zinc from body tissue, as can consuming large amounts of soda and junk foods. Copper toxicity leads to lower immune function and recurrent infections.

DETOXIFY

Lead

Neurological and psychological disturbances, including neuro-toxic effects on the brain, can be attributed to the presence of lead in the body. Lead-based solders in modern copper plumbing systems increase the amount of lead in our drinking water. As a precaution, have your water supply tested for high lead levels and filter your home water supply to remove heavy metals. Always wash your fruits and vegetables in filtered water before use. If possible, buy your produce from farms and areas that have low air pollution. Do not use any imported canned food, as the cans are often lined with lead.

Manganese

Do you cry easily? Laugh uncontrollably? It is possible that certain emotional instability can be caused by excessive levels of manganese, which are toxic to the brain's neurons. It can also contribute to muscular weakness, slowed speech and impaired equilibrium.

Manganese can be found in nuts, seeds, barley, whole grains, avocado, kidney beans, eggs, grapefruit, apricots and leaf lettuce.

Mercury

The most toxic heavy metal on earth is cadmium; mercury is second to it. One of the primary ways mercury gets into the body is through the amalgam tooth fillings that were popular for so many years. Mercury also enters the body through processed foods, drinking water, pesticides, fertilizers, mascara, floor waxes, body powder, adhesives, wood preservatives, batteries and air-conditioning filters.

FOOD ADDITIVES

There are two major categories of food additives: additives that make food more appealing to the taste buds or more pleasant to look at, and additives used to prevent food from spoiling and to increase its shelf life.

As much as 70 or 80 percent of the foods we consume is refined or altered chemically. Consumers in America use approximately 100 million pounds of food additives per year. The Federal Drug Administration (FDA) allows more than 10,000 different food and chemical additives in our food supply. The average American consumes between ten and fifteen pounds of salt and additives per year.[2] Additives commonly used include:

Aspartame

Equal and NutraSweet are brand names for the chemical aspartame. Aspartame is nearly two hundred times sweeter than sucrose and intensifies the taste of sweeteners and flavors. Research has suggested that memory loss attributed to diabetes is caused by aspartame. Large amounts of aspartame, consumed over time, cause neurotransmitter imbalance and amino acid imbalance within the body, which has a possible connection to Alzheimer's disease.

BHA (butylated hydroxyanisole)

BHA is an antioxidant that adversely affects liver and kidney function in humans. It has been associated with behavior problems in children. It is commonly used as a preservative in baked goods, candy, chewing gum, soup bases, breakfast cereals, shortening, dry mixes for desserts, potatoes, potato flakes and ice cream.

BHT (butylated hydroxytoluene)

BHT is added to food to slow rancidity in frozen and fresh pork sausage and freeze-dried meats. BHT is also found in shortening and animal fats, and it is the base product for chewing gum. Adverse effects from the use of BHT include enlargement of the liver and allergic reactions.

Caffeine

Caffeine can affect blood sugar release and increase toxicity of the liver. It stimulates the central nervous system, heart and respiration. Its ill effects include irregular heartbeat, ear noises, insomnia, irritability and nervousness.

MSG (monosodium glutamate)

Many prepared foods found on grocery shelves contain MSG, including canned tuna, snack foods and soups. It is very difficult to identify MSG on product labels because the manufacturers are not required to call it MSG. Side effects of MSG include headaches, numbness, depression, anxiety, heart palpitations and weakness. The following chart lists some of the names by which monosodium glutamate (MSG) is frequently disguised.[3]

LABEL DISGUISES FOR MSG

MSG is very frequently disguised with such names as:

- Sodium caseinate
- Hydrolyzed yeast
- Hydrolyzed vegetable protein
- Hydrolyzed protein
- Calcium caseinate
- Natural chicken (or turkey) flavoring

- Autolyzed yeast
- Textured protein
- Yeast food
- Yeast extract
- Natural flavoring
- Other spices

DETOXIFY

Phosphates

Used as a preservative, phosphates prevent outward chemical changes in food influencing texture, appearance, flavor and color. Unfortunately, phosphates also attract trace minerals in foods and then continue to remove them from the body, causing deficiencies. There are phosphates in cheese, baked goods, carbonated drinks, canned meats, powdered foods and dry cereals.

Sorbate

Sorbate is used as a fungus preventative in chocolate syrups, drinks, soda fountain syrups, baked goods, deli salads, cheesecake, fresh fruit cocktail, pie fillings, preserves and artificially sweetened jellies. It is toxic to the systems and cells of the body, and thus should be avoided.

Sulfites

Sulfites are preservatives and bleaching agents primarily used to reduce or prevent discoloration of light-colored vegetables and fruits. Sulfites release histamines and stimulate allergic reactions. They are found in sliced fruit, beer, ale, wine, packaged lemon juice, potatoes, salad dressings, gravies, corn syrup, wine vinegar, avocado dip and sauces.

WHY DETOXIFY?

As a result of this assault of harmful toxins from our foods, you may imagine that our body's filter, the liver, is constantly overworked from continuously filtering and dispelling toxins from our body. Without proper knowledge to help us give adequate maintenance to our body, we involuntarily become toxic and sick at the cellular level—that is, our cells become overloaded with toxins and cannot function properly, resulting in all kinds of illnesses.

This is the reason we are fighting for our lives, especially in America, against degenerative disease. Detoxing properly and regularly is a key to good health. Armed with this knowledge you can begin to improve your health by successfully detoxing your polluted cells.

Detoxification defined

When we perspire, urinate or defecate, we are detoxing. A slight drainage from the nose, a mouth ulcer and breaking out in a slight rash are all natural methods for the body to eliminate toxins. The healthy body is constantly working inwardly to eliminate toxic metals such as lead, mercury and aluminum.

Detoxification involves keeping all five major elimination systems functioning properly and efficiently. The five systems listed are those that need to function optimally to keep our bodies "clean":

1. The liver filters toxins and chemicals by dissipating and transforming them so they can be removed from the body.

2. The digestive tract eliminates wastes through the colon, which is basically our sewage system.

3. The kidneys are the major regulators of the water, electrolytes and acid-based content of the blood. . Indirectly, they help regulate all body fluids.

4. The skin is our largest organ. It performs its role as a barrier and our external protector. The problem here is that, due to the remarkably absorbent nature of the skin and how readily solvents and caustic chemicals can penetrate and be carried throughout the body, the skin is vulnerable to our polluted environment.

DETOXIFY

5. The lungs, along with the skin, have the greatest exposure to the environment. They work to screen foreign and harmful agents from the air we breathe continuously.

I am sure you would like for me to tell you that when your body is healthy every harmful substance can be eliminated. However, I am not sure that is possible in this toxic, "chemicalized" environment we have created for life in the twenty-first century.

Carry a 20-ounce bottle of water wherever you go.

Don't lose hope because of this statement. God's promises to help us face challenges of life apply even to the twenty-first-century health challenges. He will help us learn how to live in health as we look to Him and allow His Word to fill us with hope in His salvation. The Bible declares:

> This hope we have as an anchor of the soul, a hope both sure and steadfast and one which enters within the veil.
> —*Hebrews 6:19,* NAS

SUGGESTIONS FOR DETOXIFYING EFFICIENTLY

There are three critical steps to detoxifying and cleansing the body:

1. Water, water, water
2. Monitoring and balancing pH levels
3. Cleansing and detoxifying with food, vitamins, minerals and herbs

Water, water, water

Here are some guidelines to help you know if you are hydrating properly:

- Limit caffeine. It is a diuretic, and in too much quantity it will keep you dehydrated.

- Keep water readily available at all times. Drink a minimum of 60 ounces of water daily. I recommend that you carry a 20-ounce bottle wherever you go; it's more convenient than counting glasses. Also, if you always have it with you, it's easy to reach your daily quota.

- Begin drinking water when you wake up in the morning, and then drink a juice of your choice (for example, orange, apple or cranberry). At this point you will desire very little coffee. Good news! Your early morning quick-start will come from your newfound energy; coffee will no longer be needed for a quick-start.

- Drink a glass of water a half-hour before meals and a half-hour before your workout. You will want more water after your workout. If you establish this daily routine, you will find it extremely easy to meet your daily water quota.

- Buy a water filter for your home. It will take the impurities out of the tap water, the water will taste better and be much healthier, and the water filter is much cheaper than buying bottled water.

- Caffeinated or sugared drinks cannot be substituted for water quotas.

- Stop smoking, limit alcohol intake, and reduce caffeine intake from tea, coffee and sodas; keep in mind that staying fully hydrated will help reduce these unhealthy cravings.

- Add lemon to your water whenever convenient, especially in restaurants, as lemon is a very powerful antioxidant and will help to purify your water. Adding antioxidants always improves healthy skin, hair and internal tissues. Lemon also helps to reduce acidity and balance pH.

How water can aid your body, mind and spirit

As you commit to drinking water to hydrate your body properly, you may attest to the following health realities. (See the appendix for more information on the importance of water.)

- You may experience a possible loss of five pounds

in two weeks. Poor hydration causes you to retain fluids.

- "I don't like water" translates to "I'm addicted to caffeine, sugar, creams and other additives." Our bodies become attached to the taste and texture of what we drink.

- Water constantly cleanses and nourishes the body, assists the kidneys to function optimally, and efficiently eliminates waste.

- Cells and tissues are less likely to become toxic if they are optimally hydrated.

- Trips to the bathroom will lessen as your body adjusts to processing greater amounts of water.

- You will notice less bloating in the abdominal region, especially if you were drinking a lot of soda, and less swelling in the extremities and more comfortable-fitting clothes.

Monitoring and balancing the body's pH

An important aspect of detoxifying the body is to be aware of the pH balance. What is pH? The human body consists mainly of water, which is a biological advantage since oxygen, nutrients and biochemicals need to be transported throughout the body tissues for efficiency. Our water-based body is made up of

> "Drugs are not always necessary, [but] belief in recovery always is."
>
> **—Norman Cousins**

acid and alkaline properties, which are measured by a graduated scale called pH (potential hydrogen). The acidity and alkalinity must remain in the proper balance for a healthy state to exist in the body.

If our pH balance is consistently skewed toward either acidity or alkalinity, our health will erode drastically. Therefore, it is critically important to know what our pH balance is and to understand the biochemical balance created by vitamins, minerals, essential fatty acids, hormones and so forth.

On a scale of 1 to 10, your pH should be between 6.5 and 7.5. Some foods that cause a lower pH (more acidic) include high-protein foods (meat, fish, poultry, eggs), carbohydrates (grains, breads, pastas) and coffee. Some of the foods that cause a higher pH (more alkaline) include fresh vegetables (cucumbers, radishes, squash) and fruits (dried figs, raisins, apples, pears).

To test your pH balance, purchase pH test strips. By placing the strip into your urinary flow and then comparing the coloration on your strip to the pH scale included, you can determine your pH level at that moment. To secure a more accurate reading, repeat the test five to six times within twenty-four hours. One of these times should be the first thing in the morning before eating or drinking, which should yield your best reading since your body has all night to adjust the balance.

Below are the results of a balanced pH:

- Proper fat metabolism, weight control and healthy insulin production

- Healthy blood pressure regulation

- Efficient blood flow throughout arteries, veins and heart tissue

- Healthy cellular regeneration and DNA/RNA synthesis

- Healthy cholesterol levels, preventing plaque in arteries

- Proper electrolyte activity, which produces energy

A balanced pH also:

- Allows access to energy reserves.

- Creates a healthy oxygen flow to tissues to flush toxins.

- Promotes calcium utilization and lessens the probability of osteoporosis.

- Promotes vital lipid fatty acid and hormonal metabolism.

Cleanse and detoxify with vitamins, minerals and herbs

The following list includes cleansing and detoxing vitamins, minerals, herbs and special nutrients:

- Vitamins A, C and E are the more powerful antioxidant cleansing vitamins.

- Selenium and zinc are extremely powerful antioxidants in the form of micro-minerals. Our body doesn't need very much of either on a daily basis; however, they are essential for continuous cleansing and detoxifying.

- Scientifically designed synergistic phyto-nutrients (nutrients from plant sources) are necessary.

- Other cleansers and potent immune boosters include ginseng, gingko biloba, bee pollen and gotu kola.

Optional nutrients for cleansing and detoxing

Below is a list of supplements that you can add to your detoxification regimen. If you would like to start taking any of these items, consult with your doctor, healthcare practitioner or knowledgeable health food store specialist for dosage and product recommendations.

- Red clover and pau d'arco are extremely effective cleansing herbs for the body, especially for the liver and blood.

- Apple cider vinegar is an excellent total body and digestive track cleanser.

- Aloe vera is a total body cleanser and immune booster.

- Coenzyme Q_{10} is a powerful antioxidant for cleansing and keeping arteries clear.

- Essiac tea is also known as a total body cleanser, and I highly recommend it.[4]

- Oil of oregano is a powerful natural antiseptic.

Chlorophyll

Many foods that have high chlorophyll content are super colon cleansers and detoxifiers. Some of the most effective are the consumable grasses and algae. Three effective cleansing grasses are wheat grass, barley grass and alfalfa.

DETOXIFY

The three most effective algae are spirulina, blue-green algae and chlorella. Chlorella is very effective for detoxifying heavy metals such as mercury, lead and aluminum because it has a cracked shell and has the ability to absorb the metals.

A good cleansing habit to develop is to mix a daily "toddy" of the above grasses and algae. They can be found in ground or powder form at the health food store. Mix one scoop of your concoction with 8 ounces of purified water or juice each morning to enjoy their benefits.

Garlic and other herbs

Garlic is an absolutely wonderful cleansing herb that has antiviral, antifungal, anti-yeast and anti-parasitic properties. It is also an effective natural antibiotic. The garlic supplement with odor is my preference as it seems to be more effective.

Several other effective herbs for purifying and cleansing are red clover, echinacea, cayenne pepper, milk thistle, mullein leaf, fenugreek, burdock and goldenseal. You can find combinations of these cleansing herbs packaged for colon and other special body detoxification programs at health food stores.

I also recommend that you take a fiber supplement like those you can find at any health food store, CVS, pharmacy or Wal-Mart. Start slowly with increasing your fiber intake because it may produce bloating or excessive gas. In fact, a good way to start is with high-fiber cereal, high-fiber vegetables (like lentils, peas and beans) and whole-grain breads. Jicama (a tropical legume), pears and apples are excellent additions.

Magnesium

If ongoing constipation is causing elimination to happen only once every two or three days, a supplement for magnesium citrate should be taken. A dose of 400 milligrams, one to two capsules, three times a day will usually regulate the bowel. This wonderful mineral is also a key ingredient for fueling the energy cycle and nourishing muscle fiber and internal soft body tissue.

Vitamin C

Vitamin C is very helpful for stimulating regularity of the bowel movement. For this purpose it may be more effective to take an effervescent or buffered product such as Emergen-C. There is one caution for taking vitamin C with fiber, as fiber can bind the mineral ascorbates. If fiber binds the mineral ascorbates, they cannot be synthesized and utilized by the body. Diarrhea caused from large doses of vitamin C may be avoided by starting slow or by reducing the dosage.

Niacin (vitamin B₃)

Niacin enhances a cleansing or flushing effect in the body. Be extremely careful to start slowly in order to avoid side effects; for example, begin with 100 milligrams and increase gradually. If you decide to take larger doses for flushing, I recommend that you work with your physician so that he can monitor your liver function.

Flaxseed

Flaxseed oil is one of the better agents to battle toxicity. A tablespoon of flaxseed oil once or twice a day is a great way to help keep solvents, pesticides, insecticides and other toxins flushed out of the body. I also buy whole flaxseeds and grind them in a coffee grinder to mix with spirulina, barley grass, chlorella, wheat grass and blue-green algae for my early morning "toddy."

DETOXIFY THROUGH FASTING

Fasting is one of the most effective methods of detoxifying the body. I am a firm believer in fasting, not only for the cleansing of the body but also for the undisputed spiritual benefits it provides as well. Health benefits are a well-known product of our obedience to biblical commands to fast. The Scriptures are filled with examples of people who fasted and prayed to receive supernatural spiritual benefits. And Jesus promised a reward when we fast and pray as He taught us. He declared:

> Moreover, when you fast, do not be like the hypocrites, with a sad countenance. For they disfigure their faces that they may appear to men to be fasting. Assuredly, I say to you, they have their reward. But you, when you fast, anoint your head and wash your face, so that you do not appear to men to be fasting, but to your Father who is in the secret place; and your Father who sees in secret will reward you openly.
>
> —*Matthew 6:16–18*

Brief periods of fasting should be practiced for general health purposes. A one-day fast every month is very effective in maintaining a healthy body. Two to three days should be the maximum on a monthly basis, with one day still being the ideal. One might choose

DETOXIFY

to do a six- or seven-day fast periodically, but certainly not on a monthly basis. I have witnessed people who have attempted to fast too often for too long a period. They are in danger of losing muscle mass, compromising the immune system and becoming more vulnerable to illness, thus defeating the purpose for fasting.

Juice fasting

A juice fast is typically safer than a water fast. Great choices for a juice fast are lemon water made with freshly squeezed lemon juice or grapefruit juice. Along with juices, it is essential that you drink a minimum of 64 ounces of water on your fast day. Remember, the body is being flushed, so drink your freshly squeezed juice every three to four hours.

The juice fast is not only safer than a water fast, but it is also more efficient, enhancing the flushing of toxins. It supplies some of the daily nutrients we need, helps to prevent loss of muscle mass and is easily assimilated. For spice and variety, here are a few suggestions for periodically changing your fast routine:

1. Utilize the chlorophyll or green drink mentioned earlier with the grasses and algae. You may add flaxseed to your "toddy." Then simply drink the 64 ounces of water interspersed with your concoction, which you are drinking every three to four hours.

2. Add freshly squeezed lemon to 16 ounces of purified water. Stevia, a natural herbal sweetener, is acceptable for added taste.

3. A fresh veggie fast is very cleansing. (See my Twenty-one-Day Detoxification Program.) Munch on carrots, celery and cucumber every three to four hours. Drink your daily healthy quota of water. Additionally, you could sip on aloe vera juice periodically during the day. The aloe and green veggies are most helpful in balancing your pH (acid/alkaline) level.

4. Organic apple cider vinegar is an excellent cleanser. Add a teaspoon to 8 ounces of water and take every three to four hours.

Additional tips

Once again, I recommend that you fast one day per month. This is adequate for cleansing, and you don't risk the loss of muscle tissue. If you make a decision to fast more than one day, I recommend that you add protein to maintain muscle tissue. You can do this by adding a couple of tablespoons of protein powder such as soy, rice or whey protein to your green drinks.

To help with hunger, you can add a teaspoon of flaxseed oil to your drinks. Remember that flaxseed is cleansing, but it also gives you essential fatty acids.

You can also try different fruit and veggie drinks during your fast to keep variety in the picture. Remember to include flaxseed oil in your drinks, not only for hunger, but also for nutrition.

DR. ELROD'S TWENTY-ONE-DAY DETOXIFICATION PROGRAM

As a first step toward restoring health and wellness, I recommend that you follow my dietary guidelines for body cleansing. It will also give your immune system a new beginning. To begin, I suggest that you consider a ten-day "cooling off" period during which you gradually cut back on sugar intake as well as fat, caffeine and other unadvisable products. This ten-day period will help your body to adjust to the changes you are making and will help to ensure your success with the total program. Including the ten-day tapering off period, your cleansing (detoxification) process will be complete within thirty days. I am convinced that you will be surprised with the results, which will place you on a path to renewed health and strength and a successful lifestyle.

How to ensure success

During the twenty-one-day detoxification period, follow these guidelines to ensure that your detoxification program will be a success:

- Gradually increase your consumption of high-fiber foods:

    —Vegetables (include potatoes, spinach, tomatoes, cucumbers, radishes, carrots, red bell peppers and green leafy vegetables)

—Fresh fruits (be sure to try peaches, strawberries, grapefruit, apples, cantaloupe)

—Whole grains (such as wheat and bran cereals, whole-wheat bread, rice)

—Legumes (try lentils, beans)

—Seeds and nuts (popcorn, peanuts, sunflower seeds are all filled with fiber)

- Raw fruits and vegetables should be 50 percent of your diet.

- Be sure to drink 60 to 80 ounces of pure or distilled water daily. (Adding a lemon wedge will not only improve taste—it is also a powerful antioxidant and will help to balance your pH levels.)

- Plan your meal times, and be sure to eat moderately and deliberately. It will be important to pay attention to your meal times, so do not read or watch television while eating. (Eating while standing is a huge no-no.)

- Do NOT drink liquids while eating because they dilute the hydrochloric acid needed for digestion. Drink only acceptable liquids one hour before and two hours after meals when detoxing.

- Do not consume *less* than 1,500 calories per day during the entire twenty-one days. You should consume one-fourth of your total daily calories at breakfast, one-half of your total daily calories at lunch and the remaining one-fourth of total calories at dinner. (Do not count the two or three healthful snacks.)

- During this detoxification time, maintain a thankful heart attitude for your food, your health and all God-given blessings. Each day, visualize yourself getting well and even reaching or maintaining your ideal body weight and shape.

Things to avoid

During the ten-day tapering off period, begin eliminating the following things from your menu. Avoid them completely during the twenty-one-day program to ensure successful detoxification:

- High-fat dairy products
- White sugar and white flour
- Fried foods and junk food
- Preservatives, salt, artificial sweeteners such as aspartame (NutraSweet) and saccharin
- Red meat (especially salt-cured, smoked, nitrate-cured foods like bacon and pepperoni) and chicken (which can be high in fat). Chicken is acceptable on your regular diet.
- Coffee and caffeinated teas
- Carbonated beverages, especially sodas
- Alcoholic beverages and all forms of tobacco
- Prolonged periods of direct sun

Tips for after detox

Determine to continue eating for good health after you have successfully completed your detoxification and immune system strengthening program. Although you will not continue such a stringent nutritional program, you should follow these eating guidelines to maintain healthy living:

- Include high-fiber content in your diet (i.e., fruits, vegetables, whole grains and cereals).

- Use whole-grain foods such as whole-wheat breads, bran cereals, rice and pasta.

- Choose low-fat dairy products or dairy substitutes, like rice milk or soy milk.

- Limit red meat in your diet and eat chicken or turkey (without skin), tuna and other fish for variety.

- Emphasize fruits, vegetables and salads (with low-calorie dressings).

- Add a daily supplement of healthy omega-3 fatty acids found in fish oils and omega-6 fatty acids

DETOXIFY

found in flaxseed, olive oil, almonds and evening primrose oil.

- Limit the carbonated beverages you consume, and instead drink ten to twelve glasses of purified water per day.

DETOXIFY

DR. ELROD'S SUMMARY LIST FOR DETOXING EFFECTIVELY

- Drink a minimum of 64 ounces of purified or distilled water daily with a lemon twist.
- Decrease your intake of white sugar and flour.
- Utilize tissue-, organ-, blood- and colon-cleansing herbs.
- Limit or avoid red meats. Also avoid pork.
- Avoid the toxins of alcohol, tobacco and drugs.
- Decrease or eliminate caffeine.
- Eliminate artificial sweeteners—use Stevia.
- Increase intake of raw fruits and veggies.
- Take 1 teaspoon of apple cider vinegar with 8 ounces of water daily.
- Limit or eliminate canned, fast and refined foods.
- Increase fiber (gradually) and complex carbohydrates.
- Take 1 tablespoon of flaxseed oil daily.
- Mix equal parts of ground barley grass, wheat grass, spirulina, chlorella and blue-green algae, and take 2 tablespoons daily with juice or water.
- Fast one day per month.

Always remember, your Creator's desire for you is that you enjoy the health and prosperity for which He designed you. He wants to answer the prayer of the apostle John for you:

> Beloved, I pray that you may prosper in all things and be in health, just as your soul prospers.
>
> —*3 John 2*

DETOXIFY

CHAPTER 6

Step 3: Eat for Life

Add Years and Quality of Life

> And God said, "See, I have given you every herb
> that yields seed which is on the face of all the
> earth, and every tree whose fruit yields seed;
> to you it shall be for food."
> —GENESIS 1:29

It is vitally important that we address the nutrition issue. Why? Nutrition helps to ensure our health by equipping our immune systems to resist disease and sickness. Proper nutrition will also correct problems where disease already exists. When our systems become compromised and weakened through poor nutrition and environmental poisoning, our risk for degenerative disease and illness is significantly increased.

To function at peak performance, your body needs a variety of nutrients, including fats, carbohydrates, protein, fiber, vitamins, minerals and phytochemicals. There are a total of ninety essential nutrients required daily, including sixty minerals, sixteen vitamins, twelve essential amino acids and three essential fatty acids.

But our modern diet no longer provides all these necessary nutrients. Essential nutrients are no longer available in the soil, and the pesticides, herbicides and fertilizers we are using for agriculture cause products to be heavily laden with harmful and toxic chemicals.

Therefore, we should seek out more foods that are grown organically and possess more of the vitamins and minerals without all the added chemicals. It may also be useful to fill in any remaining gaps by taking supplements (discussed in the next chapter).

Later in this chapter, I will outline a balanced nutrition program for you that will help rebuild and maintain the immune system. I will also describe in further detail what I consider miracle nutrients. But first, let's take a closer look at dietary habits that offer the most health benefits.

ADOPT A HEALTHIER EATING LIFESTYLE

If you want to live in better health, you must adopt a healthier eating lifestyle. It is important to learn the right foods to eat—and to eat them in smaller portions than what we find on many popular "super-sized" menus. Discover the benefits of eating more frequent meals—four to six times daily—and include healthy snacks for energy and nutrition. Recognize the hazard of skipping breakfast— a habit most unhealthy and/or overweight people have developed. Use the following suggestions to help you adopt a healthier eating lifestyle:

- Eat frequently (six times a day) to avoid hunger, maintain energy and keep your metabolism operating at its optimal level.

- Include snacks in your daily routine. Choose from these nutritious snacks: raw fruits and vegetables, vegetable and fruit juices, dried fruit, whole-grain crackers, bagels, unsalted nuts, pretzels and popcorn without butter. Prevent overeating by keeping both your meals and snacks small.

- Do your best to eliminate soft drinks, candy, cookies, sugared cereals, food additives and preservatives from your diet.

- Choose foods that provide the ninety essential nutrients the body needs. Eat more fresh fruits and vegetables, seeds, nuts, cereals and whole grains. These foods are filled with necessary fiber and nutrients necessary for combating chronic disease symptoms.

NUTRITION FOR REVERSING DEGENERATIVE DISEASE

In this chapter I want to share my recommended nutrition protocol. I have designed it for your success in overcoming your battle with chronic degenerative disease. It will help you to lower the impact of damaging toxins and free radicals. You should experience less pain and inflammation as you increase the healing process in your body.

Think of your body as an intricately engineered engine with nutrition as its fuel. As you change your lifestyle and become more active, you must feed the body what it needs to restore health and healing and to regenerate your engine. A healthy lifestyle does not have to mean stringent calorie counting or restrictive dieting. You probably already know about many of these basic concepts for good nutrition. This chapter is really meant to remind you about a lot of concepts you probably already know but may have neglected to incorporate into your life.

POWER PROTEINS

Proteins should comprise 10 to 20 percent of your daily food intake. Be aware that there are several other excellent sources of protein besides meat. Many of these protein sources are higher-grade proteins than meats, and do not contain the contaminants and other problems many meats present. Your protein sources should include:

Beans

Beans, which are an excellent source of plant protein, are loaded with fiber, which helps to regulate blood sugar levels, lower blood pressure and decrease hunger. Fiber also reduces a diabetic's need for insulin.

Egg whites/egg substitutes

Eggs and egg substitutes, such as Egg Beaters, are good sources for protein. Be sure to cook eggs properly to protect against salmonella.

Fish/seafood

Choose from these excellent protein sources: perch, snapper, grouper, halibut, salmon, cod, fresh or water-packed tuna, and swordfish, grilled or baked. Shellfish like shrimp, crab and lobster are high in protein and low in fat, but be aware that shellfish are called the *scavengers of the sea.* The Bible speaks directly to this issue:

> These you may eat of all that are in the water: whatever in the water has fins and scales, whether in the seas or in the rivers—that you may eat. But all in the seas or in the rivers that do not have fins and scales, all that move in the water or any living thing which is in the water, they are an abomination to you...you shall not eat their flesh.
>
> —*Leviticus 11:9–11*

If you choose to eat shellfish, the best choices are shrimp, crab and scallops, which are generally contaminant free.

Lentils

Lentils provide B-complex vitamins and other nutrients. Studies suggest that they provide protection against heart attacks.

Poultry

Grill, bake, roast or sauté chicken or turkey breasts from which you have removed the skin. If you use ground turkey or chicken, purchase it from a butcher who uses only white meat poultry. Packaged meats may contain preservatives and additives and are less desirable. For a less traditional poultry choice, consider ostrich, which is low in fat, calories and cholesterol and tastes like beef.

Red meat

If you are struggling with a degenerative disease, it would be better if you did not include beef in your *daily* diet. However, lean beef is a super source of zinc and an immune system strengthener, and it may be used occasionally. Good beef choices include top sirloin, chuck, flank and top round cuts. Other good sources of red meat include venison (deer) and buffalo.

Skim milk

Skim milk is one of the best sources of bone-building calcium and riboflavin. Research studies reveal that when a postmenopausal woman takes 150 milligrams of calcium (in supplement form) daily, she reduces bone loss. Extra calcium can strengthen bones and prevent fractures in older adults.

Soy

Soy, a complete vegetable protein, is an important power food. Studies show that in groups where there is a high intake of soy, there are lowered rates of heart disease, osteoporosis and breast cancer.

Yogurt

Yogurt is believed to prevent allergies and colds and is a great source of calcium. Look for live cultures listed on the containers.

POWER CARBOHYDRATES

Complex carbohydrates are the body's fuel. They produce the energy you need to live life to the fullest. Simple carbohydrates such as sugars and processed sweets add empty calories to your diet and can devastate your blood sugar levels and should be avoided. But you should eat 40 to 60 percent of your daily food intake from energy-giving complex carbohydrates. Choose from the following foods:

> Carbohydrates have gotten negative attention lately, but eliminating them is not the answer.

Fruits

Rich in nutrients, fruits contain sugar in its natural form (fructose). Eating a variety of fruits will supply many necessary nutrients. Choose from the following list:

Fruit	Benefits
Apricots	Antioxidants and fiber
Bananas	Lower blood pressure, high in vitamin B_6 and potassium
Cantaloupe	Vitamin C, fiber, folic acid, potassium, beta carotene and vitamin B_6
Grapes	Source of boron, a mineral that helps to prevent osteoporosis (red grape juice

	contains resveratrol, a phyto-chemical that may help prevent heart disease by inhibiting the clumping of blood cells)
Kiwi	Vitamin C and cancer-fighting fiber
Mangos	Vitamin B_6, copper and antioxidants like beta carotene and vitamin C
Orange juice	Vitamin C and liminoids, which activate detoxifying enzymes
Pears	Vitamin C, potassium, boron and fiber
Prunes	Bone-saving boron and the antioxidant vitamins A and E
Strawberries	Offer more vitamin C and fiber than many other fruits; contain ellagic acid, a natural cancer-fighting chemical

Potatoes

A favorite carbohydrate of many—potatoes are nature made in portion sizes (choose one the size of your clenched fist). Leave off the sour cream and butter if possible.

Sweet potatoes and yams

Sweet potatoes are loaded with nutrients and are a great source of fiber. They contain nearly twice the fiber and beta carotene of white or red potatoes. They are excellent baked, boiled or microwaved. Store them in a dry, cool place. If you refrigerate them, they become hard and bitter tasting.

Whole grains

Whole-grain foods are rich in vitamin B_6, fiber and manganese. Choose from the following list:

Whole-grain food	Benefits
Barley	Low glycemic index score, one of the healthiest carbohydrate foods available
Bran cereal	High in wheat bran and insoluble fiber
Brown rice	Burns much slower than white rice, producing more energy longer, provides thiamine, niacin, copper and zinc
Pasta	Not a whole grain, but is a low glycemic index food
Oatmeal	Lowers LDL (bad) cholesterol
Wheat germ	Fiber, magnesium, manganese, chromium, zinc, iron, vitamin E and B-complex vitamins
Whole-wheat bread	Choose unprocessed, whole-grain bread

EAT FOR LIFE

Be careful about your choice of carbohydrates. My research and experience over more than twenty-five years have indicated that carbohydrates *are not the culprits* in our diets that some popular diets suggest. Avoid refined carbohydrates and sugars. As I explained in my book *Reversing Fibromyalgia,* "the determining factor is the rapidity with which carbohydrates are broken down into glucose, or ready-to-use blood sugar, as our primary fuel source."[1]

Nutrition scientists use a rating scale called the *glycemic index* to rank foods on a scale of 0 to 100, depending on how fast they are digested and converted to glucose. The chart below shows the scores for some popular carbohydrates. Emphasize low-scoring glycemic index foods in your diet, but be reminded that you can also have some high glycemic index foods if eaten in moderation. For more information, refer to the book *The New Glucose Revolution* by Jennie Brand-Miller.[2]

EAT FOR LIFE

GLYCEMIC INDEX SCORES FOR CARBOHYDRATES

Food	Score	Food	Score
Barley	25	Popcorn	55
Grapefruit	25	Rice, brown	55
Kidney beans	27	Apricot	57
Lentils	30	Bread,	57
Fettuccine	32	whole-wheat pita	
Apple	38	Rice, basmati	58
Pear	38	Potato, new	62
Peach	42	Raisins	64
Orange	44	Cantaloupe	65
Grapes, green	46	Couscous	65
Linguine	46	Bread,	69
Bulgur	48	whole wheat	
(cracked wheat)		Bread, white	70
Oatmeal	49	Bagel	72
(rolled oats)		Graham crackers	74
Bread, 100% stone	53	Rice cakes	82
ground whole wheat		Pretzels	83
Buckwheat	54	Corn flakes	84
Sweet potato	54	Potato, baked	85
Corn	55	Rice, white, instant	87

POWER VEGETABLES

Vegetables are packed with nutrients and antioxidants, and are low in calories. One study found a link between vegetable consumption and rheumatoid arthritis risk, and another found that a vegetable diet may reduce incidence of joint pain.[3]

Remember that cheese and butter *are not part of your vegetables!* Buy veggies fresh or frozen and eat as many of them as possible. Raw fruits and veggies are some of the best cleansers and detoxifiers. Choose from the following list of healthy vegetables:

Vegetable	Benefits
Broccoli	Potassium and chromium, which stabilize blood sugar; filled with fiber, vitamin C, beta carotene, bone-building calcium, folic acid, boron and sulforaphane, which detoxifies harmful enzymes in the body
Cabbage	Substances called indoles in cabbage are anticancer agents
Carrots	Beta carotene
Garlic	Protects against heart disease and stroke, may lower blood pressure and acts as a natural antibiotic
Kale	Fiber, calcium, manganese, vitamin B_6, copper and potassium; reduces the harmful effects of LDL cholesterol
Pumpkin	High in beta carotene and fiber
Red bell peppers	Antioxidant properties; inhibit the formation of carcinogenic nitrosamines (from foods containing nitrates)
Spinach	A powerhouse of antioxidants and rich in folic acid
Tomatoes	Contain lycopene, thought to prevent some cancers; also an excellent source of vitamins A and C, fiber and potassium

EAT FOR LIFE

POWER FATS

Not all fats are bad. There is no need to eliminate *all* fats from your diet. There are good fats and bad fats, with saturated fats and trans fats being the worst. Unsaturated fats in moderate amounts are actually good for you. Good fats include olive oil, canola oil, omega-3 fish oil, sesame oil, flaxseed oil and evening primrose oil.

About 1 tablespoon a day of these good fats provides your body with all the essential fatty acids it needs. Include the following *good fats* in your diet:

Oil	Benefits
Fish oil	Contains essential fatty acids (EFAs), which lower triglycerides
Nuts	Provide omega-6 fatty acids, which help keep the coronary arteries clear and cholesterol at healthy levels[4]
Olive oil	Oil richest in monounsaturated fats
Sunflower seeds	High in vitamin E, an antioxidant that fights heart disease, cancer and cataracts
Grape seed oil	Powerful antioxidant, fifty times stronger than tocopherol (known forms of vitamin E) and twenty times stronger than vitamin C

At least two other foods deserve mention here for the powerful way they can contribute to your health. *Ginger* is a spice and, like many other spices (including rosemary, pepper, oregano and thyme), is a powerful antioxidant. Green and black teas have tremendous health benefits. They are an excellent alternative to coffee.

PLANNING FOR SUCCESS

Healthy, high-nutrient meals do not have to be tasteless, bland and boring. If you follow my program, meals can be tasty, fun and energizing. I have included some meal-planning ideas and charts to help you organize your new regimen. (See Part IV.) Here are a few more suggestions to help you plan your healthy nutritional program:

- *Snack options*—Fresh veggies or fruit, yogurt with granola or low-fat cottage cheese with fruit, unsalted nuts, healthy trail mixes, a small tuna fish sandwich on whole-wheat bread, a freshly made fruit or veggie juice or smoothie.

- *Plan in advance*—Try a nutritional drink or bar for one or two of your meals on your busiest days. Soy drinks or powder shakes are tasty and nutritious. Make smoothies or other health drinks by adding fruit, fruit juice, soy powder, wheat germ or other health additives.

- *Make a list*—Always make a list before going to the grocery store. Use the list of power foods on pages 75–82 to help you plan ahead so that you will consistently eat better. Meal planning ensures your success in sticking with a healthy diet and reversing degenerative diseases.

- *Take a "day of rest"*—Follow the plan I outline for six days a week, and then take a day of rest from the plan when you can eat anything and everything that you wish. This day will remind you of what it feels like to overeat, stuff yourself, become sluggish, have an energy drain and indigestion—all the things created by overeating and eating improperly. You will more readily return to sensible eating.

- *Meal, water, supplements planners*—Part IV contains meal, water and supplements planners (forms) so you can plan all six meals each day ahead of time. There are also slots to check off where you are consistently taking your nutrients and drinking adequate amounts of water. When you can see these results, it will give you some sense of satisfaction that you are staying on track and accomplishing your goals, not to mention the fact that you are assuring yourself that you have the proper amount and proportions of carbohydrates, protein, healthy fats and veggies.

EAT FOR LIFE

SUMMARY: IMPROVING YOUR QUALITY OF LIFE

I trust you have read these pages carefully, highlighting the specific foods you want to incorporate into your more nutritional dietary regimen. It is possible to acquire a taste for new foods, as well, that you have not tried, especially when your body is appropriately detoxified and you are eating for energy and health.

Simplicity is the key to succeeding in your pursuit of health. Don't try to initiate every new idea you have read all at once, but like a good student, continue to refer to the dos and don'ts you have read. Expect to feel better as you incorporate more of the dos.

As we continue on our journey toward an improved quality of life, I want to introduce you to the need for supplementing your diet of good fresh foods with vitamins, minerals and other supplements that I call miracle nutrients. For chronic disease sufferers, these special nutrients can impact your health so powerfully that it will seem as if you have received a miracle. As you commit to detoxifying your body and then replenishing it with the foods we have recommended, you will aid your healing by adding some of these important nutrients.

EAT FOR LIFE

CHAPTER 7

Step 4: Supplement for Efficiency

Vitamins, Minerals and the Miracle Nutrients

> **The heart of the wise teaches his mouth, and adds learning to his lips. Pleasant words are like a honeycomb, sweetness to the soul and health to the bones.**
>
> —PROVERBS 16:23–24

Let's assume that you have achieved your goal of balance and variety with your Body Advantage Eating for Life Program. Nutrition has become your forte, and you are consuming a wide variety of fruits, vegetables and fish twice a week, using olive and grape seed oils on salads sprinkled with sunflower and flaxseeds. Finally, you are eating smaller but healthier portions six times a day.

Now that you are regularly choosing to cultivate this healthy eating lifestyle, you may wonder why the need for a chapter about nutritional supplements. That is a good question, and the answer is quite simple. As we age, the immune system becomes compromised and slows down due to our lifestyles as well as exposure to environmental toxins. As the body becomes toxic, the immune system becomes less capable of producing adequate T cells and natural killer (NK) cells to fight off the harmful invaders known as antigens. T cells are immune cells produced in the thymus gland to help fight the battle against invading organisms in the body.

Even at younger ages, the immune system needs extra boosting in the form of vitamins and minerals to assist with the harmful effects of stress, environmental toxins, sleep deprivation and less than adequate diet and exercise programs. Dr. Ramjit Kumar Chandra, M.D., Ph.D., director of the World Health Organization's Center for Nutritional Immunology in St. John's, Newfoundland, has done studies supporting the fact that after only a few weeks of good nutrition and appropriate supplements, the immune system improves significantly.[1]

There are many nutrients that can help the body to strengthen its immune system and be restored to health that even the best diet may not furnish fully. Vitamins, minerals and herbal supplements are needed along with our food to provide the balance and variety needed for a strong, adequate immune system to correct degenerative disease and then to maintain good health.

THE VALUE OF MINERALS

Minerals are essential for proper nutrition and health. Minerals are absolutely the most important of all the body's nutrients. Even though the body needs only small amounts of many minerals, they need to be supplied on a daily basis to maintain and regulate necessary body functions. There are eighty-four known minerals, twenty-two of those being essential. If there is a shortage of one or more, the balance of the body's systems can be thrown off. Let's take a closer look at some of the benefits of these essential nutrients:

- They provide for the healthy development and function of the body.
- Without minerals, vitamins, amino acids, enzymes, fats and carbohydrates cannot be absorbed and utilized by the body.
- Minerals normalize the heartbeat.
- They improve the brain and mental abilities.
- They stabilize the nervous system.
- The proper level of minerals increases energy and fights fatigue.
- Electrolyte levels are balanced by minerals.
- Minerals assist the metabolic process.
- They assist in the regulation of the delicate balance

SUPPLEMENTS

of body fluids. They are vitally important in the process of osmosis, which includes emptying the body of waste and bringing oxygen and nutrients to the cells.

In essence, minerals are essential for all mental and physical functions.

Mineral deficiency promotes disease.

As minerals disappear from our soils and food supply, more and more people suffer from mineral deficiencies. Most of our required minerals used to be available through our diet. But as our food supplies have become more and more "refined," and as large quantities of chemicals and toxins are added to our soil as the result of "modern technology," minerals are disappearing from our food supply faster than updated charts can be published. We can no longer rely on obtaining sufficient quantities of essential minerals from our food alone. Plants that are deficient in minerals also tend to be deficient in vitamins and in protein.

Compounding the problem of our nutrient-deficient food supply is the fact that our lifestyles today are filled with undue stress and emotional disruption—two more causes of deficiency of some minerals, especially magnesium. Research has proven that extended periods of stress and anxiety result in mineral imbalances, and this appears to be one of the primary factors that promotes the onset of degenerative diseases. Mineral deficiency results in a nutritional imbalance that can also lead to a disruption of sleep patterns, concentration and the ability to interact normally.[2]

If you are still not convinced about the need for supplements, consider data from the USDA that found that approximately half of the U.S. population regularly consumes a diet deficient in basic RDA nutrients.[3] In other words, Americans are typically not consuming the minimum RDA recommendations in one or more minerals each day. On top of that, the RDAs are only meant to prevent malnutrition; they do not give dosage amounts for optimal daily nutrition.

In this section I am listing some of the important minerals and their nutritional value for those who suffer from degenerative diseases. For many of the minerals, I have included the mineral's benefits, symptoms of deficiency and the recommended dosage.

SUPPLEMENTS

Calcium

Calcium is the most abundant mineral needed by the body. Most of the calcium in the body is located in the bones and the teeth.

> *Benefits:* Calcium is necessary for the transmission of nerve signals, the smooth functioning of the heart muscles and the muscular movements of the intestines. It has a calming effect in the body and is very effective if taken before bedtime to help relax muscles and promote sleep.
>
> *Symptoms of deficiency:* Some of the symptoms of a calcium deficiency are tingling of the lips, fingers and feet, leg numbness, muscle cramps and sensitivity to noise. If a deficiency of calcium is allowed, the blood will leech calcium out of the bones, enhancing osteoporosis.
>
> *Recommended dosage:* 500 milligrams daily. A powdered calcium supplement should be taken daily. Calcium should be balanced with magnesium for proper nerve function and for a healthy body. Magnesium, phosphorous, zinc and vitamins A, C and D must be taken in combination with calcium for the calcium to be absorbed and to function efficiently. Do not take antacids to make up for calcium deficiency.

Chromium

> *Benefits:* Chromium is essential for the synthesis of fatty acids and the metabolism of blood sugars for energy. It is also known for increasing the efficiency of insulin in carbohydrate metabolism.
>
> *Symptoms of deficiency:* Weight gain, glucose intolerance and psychological confusion.
>
> *Recommended dosage:* 200 micrograms daily.

Iodine

> *Benefits:* Very little of the trace mineral iodine is required by the body, but it is essential for the thyroid

SUPPLEMENTS

hormone thyroxine. When supported by iodine, the thyroid gland helps to facilitate energy production.

Symptoms of deficiency: A malfunctioning thyroid can cause symptoms of fatigue and lethargy. Other symptoms of iodine deficiency are swollen fingers and toes, dry hair, cold hands and feet and irritability. Too much iodine also negatively affects the thyroid gland.

Iron

Many people still suffer from an iron deficiency. Iron is not easily absorbed by the body and requires an adequate amount of hydrochloric acid for proper assimilation. Vitamins C and E are also necessary if iron is to be utilized efficiently.

Benefits: Iron is known as the anti-anemia mineral because of its assistance in the oxygenation of cells and combining with protein to form hemoglobin.

Magnesium

Magnesium is a major regulator of cellular activity, including the maintenance of DNA and RNA. It is also considered an anti-stress mineral.

Benefits: Magnesium has a calming effect and is effective when taken before bedtime. It is an essential part of the enzyme system but is poorly assimilated by the body, so it should be taken daily by the chronic disease sufferer. This important mineral assists in the absorption of potassium, calcium, phosphorus, sodium and B-complex vitamins as well as vitamins C and E.

Symptoms of deficiency: Magnesium deficiencies are often caused by stress, malabsorption, diarrhea, diabetes and kidney disease. A chocolate craving is sometimes indicative of a magnesium deficiency. Other symptoms of deficiency include weakness, depression, apprehension, irritability in the nerves and muscles, nausea, vomiting, sensitivity to noise, muscle cramps and insomnia.

SUPPLEMENTS

Recommended dosage: 200–400 milligrams daily. Magnesium should be taken with calcium. Note: Heart patients and expectant mothers should check with their physician before taking magnesium.

Manganese

Benefits: Manganese is found in many enzymes in the body and assists in the utilization of glucose. It also aids in reproduction and the normal functioning of the central nervous system. It is vital for proper brain function, muscles and nerves and is very important for energy production.

Symptoms of deficiency: Nausea, dizziness, muscle coordination problems, strained knees, loss of hearing, low cholesterol and slow growth of hair and nails.

Recommended dosage: 4 milligrams daily.

Phosphorus

Phosphorus and calcium work together and are found mainly in the bones and teeth. Phosphorus levels can be decreased by drinking too many sodas, by a deficiency of vitamin D and by stress.

Benefits: Phosphorus is essential for chronic disease sufferers because it helps to produce energy as it aids in the oxidation of carbohydrates.

Symptoms of deficiency: Loss of appetite, irregular breathing, nervous disorder and insomnia.

Recommended dosage: 200 milligrams daily.

Potassium

Benefits: Potassium is responsible for normal heart and muscle function, normal transmission of nerve impulses and normal growth. It works with sodium to regulate the flow of nutrients in and out of the cells, and it also helps to stimulate the kidneys, keep the adrenals healthy and maintain heart rhythm. Potassium is vital in stimulating nerve impulses that cause muscle contraction.

Symptoms of deficiency: The symptoms of a potassium deficiency include muscle twitches, weakness and soreness, erratic rapid heartbeats, fatigue, glucose intolerance, nervousness, high cholesterol and insomnia.

Recommended dosage: 100 milligrams daily.

Selenium

Selenium is considered an aid to other nutrients, especially vitamin E.

Benefits: Selenium is a very powerful antioxidant and is needed for immune function, cell membrane integrity and DNA metabolism. It protects the body from drug and heavy metal toxins (aluminum, cadmium and mercury).

Recommended dosage: 100 micrograms daily.

Vanadium

Vanadium is commonly believed to be essential in preventing heart disease.

Benefits: Vanadium is a cofactor to insulin and, along with chromium, is very efficient in breaking down fats and sugars, which helps to keep coronary arteries clear. This mineral is vital in the creation of energy. Diabetics would do well to take both chromium and vanadium to assist with the utilization of insulin.

Recommended dosage: 20 milligrams daily.

Zinc

Zinc is a vital component of enzymes in the brain that repair cells. Vitamin A must be present for zinc to be absorbed properly by the body.

Benefits: Zinc is very important for hearing, vision and taste. It helps to form skin, hair and nails. Zinc also assists with the absorption of vitamins in the body and is essential for the many enzymes involved in digestion and metabolism.

SUPPLEMENTS

Symptoms of deficiency: Depression, distorted taste sensation, diarrhea, brittle nails and hair, hair loss, fatigue and memory loss.

Recommended dosage: 30 milligrams daily.

A LOOK AT VITAMINS

Vitamins are necessary for life and good health. They are constantly used in the body, and many of them need to be replaced daily. As with minerals, today it is often difficult to obtain enough vitamins from our food supply alone, and we must maintain normal levels by taking vitamin supplements. Many people with systemic conditions suffer from vitamin deficiencies.

Vitamins are necessary for the body to utilize other nutrients. Some vitamins also contribute to breaking down fats. The fat-soluble vitamins are A, D, K and E. They combine with the fats to be absorbed in the body and remain in the body for a much longer period of time.

Water-soluble vitamins are broken down and assimilated by water. Fat-soluble vitamins (A, D, K and E) cannot be broken down by water and can build up a toxic effect if overloaded.

Vitamins should normally be taken before meals in order for proper absorption to take place.

Vitamin A

Vitamin A is a fat-soluble vitamin; it can be toxic if taken in large quantities because it remains stored in the fat of the body. Beta carotene is nontoxic, however, and is converted to vitamin A in the body on an as-needed basis. Therefore it is recommended that you supplement with beta carotene to maintain adequate vitamin A levels in the body.

Benefits: Vitamin A helps maintain and repair muscle tissue, treats skin problems, fights infection and aids in the growth and maintenance of healthy bones, skin, teeth and gums.

Sources: Yellow and green vegetables, eggs, milk, liver, fish liver oils, carrots, apricots and sweet potatoes.

Symptoms of deficiency: Dry hair, itchy and burning eyes, sinus trouble and fatigue.

Recommended dosage: 5,000–15,000 IU of beta carotene daily. It is safe to take up to 25,000 IU of beta carotene on a daily basis without a toxic effect.

B-complex vitamins

Because chronic disease patients are under a great deal of stress from illness, they need more B vitamins.

Benefits: B vitamins assist in the calming process and in establishing good mental health. They are also vital in the production of serotonin, a chemical in the body that influences calming behavior. B-complex vitamins work together to calm the nervous system and support correct brain function, as well as to improve concentration and memory.

Symptoms of deficiency: A deficiency of B vitamins due to inadequate nutrition or increased demand can significantly contribute to the lack of ability to handle stress.

Recommended dosage: Consider the recommended dosages for each of the individual B vitamins in the list below. Much care should be taken with dosages of the B vitamins. There are good vitamin B complexes available that ensure proper balance.

Vitamin B$_1$ (thiamine)

Benefits: Vitamin B$_1$ is necessary for digestion, blood cell metabolism, muscle metabolism, pain inhibition and energy.

Sources: Rice bran, wheat germ, oatmeal, whole wheat, sunflower seeds, brewer's yeast and peanuts. Herbs that contain vitamin B$_1$ are gotu kola, kelp, peppermint, slippery elm and ginseng.

Recommended dosage: 25 milligrams daily. It is a water-soluble vitamin and is needed in small amounts on a daily basis.

SUPPLEMENTS

Vitamin B$_2$ (riboflavin)

Benefits: Necessary for formation of antibodies and red blood cells, cell respiration, and fat and carbohydrate metabolism. It is also essential for proper enzyme formation, normal growth and tissue formation.

Sources: Wild rice, liver, fish, white beans, sesame seeds, wheat germ and red peppers. A few of the herbs containing B$_2$ are gotu kola, kelp, peppermint and ginseng.

Recommended dosage: 25 milligrams daily. Vitamin B$_2$ is water soluble and must be replaced on a daily basis.

Vitamin B$_3$ (niacinamide)

Benefits: Assists the body in producing insulin, female and male hormones, and thyroxine. Vitamin B$_3$ is also needed for circulation, acid production and histamine activation.

Sources: White meat, avocados, whole wheat, prunes, liver and fish.

Symptoms of deficiency: Hypoglycemia, memory loss, irritability, confusion, diarrhea, ringing in the ears, depression and insomnia.

Recommended dosage: 25 milligrams daily.

Vitamin B$_5$ (pantothenic acid)

Benefits: Vital for the normal functioning of muscle tissue. It protects membranes from infection. It is essential for energy conversion, blood stimulation and detoxification. Individuals under excessive stress and/or with poor diets need pantothenic acid to assist in normal body functioning.

Symptoms of deficiency: Digestive problems, muscle pain, fatigue, depression, irritability and insomnia. Supplementation is vital for degenerative disease sufferers because of the muscle pain, fatigue and depression related to a deficiency of pantothenic acid.

Recommended dosage: 10 milligrams daily.

Vitamin B₆ (pyridoxine)

Benefits: Helpful in converting fats and proteins into energy and with the production of red blood cells. It is also essential for proper chemical balance in the body.

Symptoms of deficiency: Irritability, nervousness, depression, muscle weakness, pain, headaches, PMS and stiff joints.

Recommended dosage: 20 milligrams daily. Too much vitamin B_6 can cause a folic acid deficiency.

Vitamin B₁₂ (cobalamin)

Benefits: Essential for iron absorption and for fat, protein and carbohydrate metabolism. It aids in the formation of blood cells and cell longevity. A strict vegetarian will need vitamin B_{12} supplements.

Symptoms of deficiency: Headaches, memory loss, dizziness, paranoia, muscle weakness, fatigue and depression.

Recommended dosage: 200 micrograms daily.

Biotin

Benefits: Especially needed if you are under excessive stress, are experiencing malabsorption or have a poor nutrition program. Biotin aids in protein, fat and carbohydrate metabolism, fatty acid production and cell growth.

Symptoms of deficiency: Muscle pain, nausea, anemia, fatigue, high cholesterol and depression.

Recommended dosage: 200 micrograms daily.

SUPPLEMENTS

Vitamin C (ascorbic acid)

Benefits: Helps prevent infection by increasing the activity of white blood cells and assists in destroying viruses and bacteria. It also performs as a powerful antioxidant and is considered an anti-stress vitamin. It is essential for healing and the synthesis of neuro-transmitters in the brain. When combined with bioflavonoids, it also assists with adrenal and immune functions. It helps in the formation of col-lagen, which is essential for good skin, bones, teeth and growth in children.

Symptoms of deficiency: The following conditions usually call for an increase in vitamin C: infections, fevers, injuries, excessive physical activity, anemia and cortisone use.

Sources: Citrus fruits, cantaloupe, vegetables, broc-coli, cauliflower and red and green peppers. Some herbs that are good vitamin C sources are hawthorn berries, passionflower, olive oil, ginseng and horsetail.

Recommended dosage: 1,000 milligrams daily (min-imum). Vitamin C is a water-soluble vitamin needing to be replaced daily.

Vitamin E (tocopherol)

Benefits: Vitamin E helps control the unsaturated fats in the body and is thought to reduce cholesterol. It helps to normalize brain function and protects glands during stress. It is a powerful antioxidant. It is needed for cholesterol metabolism, blood clotting, lung metabolism, muscle and nerve maintenance, and body cleansing.

Sources: Peanuts, vegetable oils, lettuce, wheat germ, whole grains, spinach, corn and egg yolks. The herb kelp is also a good source of vitamin E.

Recommended dosage: 400–800 IU daily.

SUPPLEMENTS

Vitamin P (bioflavonoids)

Benefits: Work together with vitamin C to strengthen connective tissue and capillaries. Bioflavonoids are also essential to assist the body in utilizing most of the other nutrients.

Sources: Spinach, cherries, rose hips, citrus fruits, apricots, blackberries and grapes. Herbs that contain bioflavonoids are paprika and rose hips.

Recommended dosage: 250–1,000 milligrams daily.

PABA (para aminobenzoic acid)

Benefits: PABA assists in facilitating protein metabolism and in promoting growth and blood cell formation.

Symptoms of deficiency: Depression, fatigue, irritability, nervousness, constipation and eventually arthritis.

Recommended dosage: 200 micrograms daily.

HERBS ARE CATALYSTS

Since the beginning of time, nature has provided mankind with herbs that have been used as healing agents. Although herbs have been used for healing since ancient times, it is only recently that modern technology has recognized that all the chemical elements contained in the leaves, roots, bark, fruits and flowers of herbs are the same chemicals that make up the human body.

Herbs contain hormones, enzymes, vitamins, minerals, essential fatty acids, chlorophyll, fiber and many other important elements. They provide the body with important nutrients needed to boost the immune system and to aid the body in healing itself. They are most effective when used in their natural, balanced state. The body appears to be able to utilize herbs when and where they are needed, and naturalists believe the body is readily able to receive and assimilate their nutrients.

Herbs almost always contain elements in the amounts that nature intended. Herbalists believe that using herbs can add health and vigor to the body because herbs provide a broad array of catalysts that work together synergistically and harmoniously, resulting in the complete healing of the body in most cases.

Drugs made synthetically from plants are no longer in their natural form, and people often find that these drugs cause more harm than good because of side effects. In contrast, herbs are natural and safe, usually without causing side effects. Still, herbs need to be used with wisdom and knowledge. They should not be used or mixed with other medications unless directed by a physician.

Because no one single herb contains the proper healing qualities required to treat symptoms, herbal combinations are generally formulated to complement one another. By combining several herbs together, formulas are able to treat many symptoms that a single herb cannot.

Below are some herbs and natural nutrients that may be of benefit to those with degenerative disease and other systemic conditions:

Aloe vera

Although the aloe vera plant looks like a cactus, it is actually a member of the lily family. Aloe vera is high in vitamin C and selenium, two powerful antioxidants that help prevent and cure diseases. It also contains vitamin A, B-complex vitamins, phosphorus, magnesium, potassium, niacin, manganese and zinc.

> *Benefits:* Promotes healing when used externally and is effective for treating radiation burns. Increases movement in the intestines, promotes menstruation, relieves constipation and aids in digestion. It helps to eliminate toxins in the body and is used very effectively to treat inflammation and ulcers. It contains salicylic acid and magnesium, which function together as an analgesic.

Chamomile

Ancient Egyptians used chamomile for its healing properties. It contains vitamins A, C, F (linoleic acid and alpha-linoleic acid) and B complex, which are also effective for the nervous system. Selenium and zinc, significant for the immune system, are also found in chamomile. Finally, the herb contains tryptophan, the component that allows it to work as a sedative and promote sleep.

SUPPLEMENTS

Benefits: Chamomile possesses relaxing properties that are very effective in promoting relaxation and inducing sleep. It also promotes digestion and assists in assimilating nutrients from food, thereby enhancing metabolism and the utilization of energy.

Echinacea

Echinacea is a very powerful nutrient that stimulates the immune response in the body and assists the body in increasing its ability to resist infection. It assists in the promotion of white blood cells and is a blood purifier. Native Americans used echinacea for snakebites, insect stings and infections.

Benefits: Echinacea is a natural antibiotic. Extracts of echinacea root have been found to contain interferon-like properties. Interferon is produced naturally in the body to prevent viral infections and has been known to fight chemical toxic poisoning in the body. Echinacea contains vitamin C, which helps to promote healing and fights infections. Calcium and vitamin E are also found in this powerful herb. Echinacea contains iodine, which assists the thyroid gland in regulating metabolism, mental development and energy production. It also contains potassium for muscle contraction, kidney function and nerve function. The sulfur content of echinacea helps to dissolve acids in the body and improve circulation.

Ginseng

Ginseng has been rated as the most potent of herbs because it supports so many body functions.

Benefits: Helps the heart and circulation, normalizes blood pressure and prevents arteriosclerosis. It is used to protect the body against radiation and as an antidote to drugs and toxic chemicals. The roots are effective against bronchitis and heart disease. It reduces blood cholesterol, improves brain function and memory, increases physical stamina, stimulates the endocrine glands, strengthens the central nervous system and builds the immune system.

SUPPLEMENTS

Goldenseal

Benefits: Boosts a sluggish glandular system and promotes hormone production. It goes directly into the blood stream and assists in regulating liver function. It also acts as a natural form of insulin, thus aiding metabolism and energy production. Goldenseal may also act as a natural antibiotic to stop infections. Goldenseal is a very powerful immune booster. This herb contains vitamins A, C, E, F and B complex. It also contains potassium, phosphorus, iron, calcium, zinc and manganese.

Gotu kola

Benefits: Helps with mental fatigue and memory loss. Naturalists recommend gotu kola for rejuvenating the nervous system. It is sometimes referred to as "brain food" because of its ability to energize brain function. It is also used to increase circulation, neutralize blood toxins, help balance hormones and relax the nerves. Gotu kola is rich in magnesium; it also contains vitamins A, C and K, which protect the lungs and the immune system from diseases. Vitamin K is necessary for blood clotting and in healing colitis. Gotu kola is a good source of manganese, niacin, zinc, calcium, sodium, and vitamins B_1 and B_2.

Herbal teas for relief

There are a number of delicious herbal teas that are excellent alternatives to soft drinks and bottled fruit juices, which are both normally loaded with sugar. Try herbal teas such as chamomile, spearmint, peppermint, cinnamon, orange peel and valerian root. You can drink the tea hot or chilled, or you can make it into ice by pouring it into molds and freezing it.

Benefits: A calming and soothing combination tea for help in inducing sleep is passionflower, valerian, hops and chamomile. Drink the tea half an hour before bed. Green herbal teas are especially helpful, particularly for strengthening the immune system.

SUPPLEMENTS

Passionflower

> *Benefits:* Has properties that are helpful for the nerves and circulation. Passionflower works well in formulas designed to treat insomnia and to combat nervous tension, anxiety, stress, restlessness and nervous headaches. It is helpful for fevers.

Pau d'arco

> *Benefits:* Reported to be a natural blood cleanser and builder, pau d'arco also possesses antibiotic properties, which aid in destroying viral infections in the body. It helps combat cancer and has been used to strengthen the body, increase energy and strengthen the immune system.

Red clover

This herb is high in vitamin A and is an excellent choice in any tea blend since it is usually more effective when complemented with other herbs. Some of the herbs complementary to red clover are prickly ash bark, echinacea, cascara sagrada bark, rosemary and buckthorn bark.

> *Benefits:* A natural blood purifier and builder, red clover is normally used in its liquid form. It protects the immune system and gives the body energy, as well as contains some antibiotic properties that are beneficial against bacteria.[4] This herb has been used for treating bronchitis, cancer and nervous conditions and for removing toxins from the body. It is invaluable to the degenerative disease sufferer because it is high in selenium, which is very important in the nutritional regimen, and because it also contains manganese, sodium, calcium, copper, magnesium and B-complex vitamins. Red clover contains vitamin C as well, which is necessary for boosting the immune system and preventing disease.

Rosemary

> *Benefits:* Rosemary often replaces aspirin for the treatment of headaches, as well as combats stress and

SUPPLEMENTS

improves memory. It is considered of benefit to the entire nervous system.

Slippery elm

Benefits: Buffers against irritations and inflammations of the mucous membranes. A very powerful nutrient for degenerative sufferers, it assists the activity of the adrenal glands and is a nutritious herb for both internal and external healing. It has been used primarily to treat stomach and intestinal ulcers, gastrointestinal problems, digestion acidity and to lubricate the bowels. Slippery elm is a blood builder and supports the cardiovascular system.

Valerian

Valerian is probably the herb most widely used for anxiety and nervous tension. It is used as a natural sedative to improve sleep and relieve insomnia. Valerian contains essential oils and alkaloids that reportedly combine to produce its calming, sedative effect.

Benefits: Used to combat depression, for after-pains in childbirth, heart palpitations, muscle spasms and arthritis. Valerian is rich in calcium, which accounts for its ability to strengthen the spine, nerves and brain. It is also high in magnesium, which works with calcium for healthy bones and nervous system, and in selenium and manganese to strengthen the immune system, as well as zinc and vitamins A and C.

MIRACLE NUTRIENTS

There are some nutrients that I consider "miracle nutrients," and I recommend them in rebuilding and maintenance programs for chronic degenerative disease sufferers. These nutrients are wonderfully healing to degenerative disease conditions. Some of these have been listed in the previous listings, but I'm grouping them together here for emphasis.

Apple cider vinegar

Benefits: One of the best total body purifiers and

SUPPLEMENTS

cleansers, it is most effective when used in its organic form.

Recommended use: It is usually a very potent formula and is best tolerated mixed with a healthy juice or purified water.

Bee pollen

Bee pollen is very high in protein and is considered one of the most complete foods that we can consume. It contains vitamins, minerals, amino acids, proteins, enzymes and fats.

Benefits: It helps when there is a hormone imbalance in the body. It helps to increase appetite, normalize intestinal activity, strengthen capillary walls, offset the effects of drugs and pollutants and is one of the most powerful immune boosters known to man.

Beta carotene

There are dozens of carotenoids (red and yellow plant and animal pigments), including beta carotene, the plant form of vitamin A.

Sources: Yellow and orange fruits and vegetables such as carrots, cantaloupe, sweet potatoes, pumpkin, apricots, mango, papaya, peaches and winter squash. Dark green leafy vegetables such as collard greens, parsley, spinach, broccoli and other leafy greens are other excellent sources of beta carotene.

Boron

Benefits: Possesses antioxidant functions and is very important in maintaining muscular health.

Chondroitin sulfates

Benefits: Naturally occurring substances that inhibit the enzymes that can degrade cartilage and help to attract fluid to proteoglycan molecules.

Chromium

Benefits: Essential for the synthesis of fatty acids and the metabolism of glucose for energy. It is also

SUPPLEMENTS

well known for its ability to increase the efficiency of insulin.

Coenzyme Q_{10}

Benefits: The discovery of coenzyme Q_{10} is of tremendous benefit to mankind. It compares with vitamins A, C and E as a powerful antioxidant. Coenzyme Q_{10} fights diseases associated with nutrient deficiencies such as cancer, aging, heart disease, obesity and fibromyalgia. This nutrient aids in the oxygenation of cells and tissues, boosts biochemical ability and activates cellular energy while improving circulation. One research study found that coenzyme Q_{10} literally doubled the immune system's ability to clear invading organisms from the blood.[5]

Sources: Found in food sources such as spinach, sardines and peanuts.

Colostrum

Benefits: When our immune cells become more efficient, we can more readily combat chronic systemic conditions. Colostrum is a transfer factor that is a vital immune booster; it educates immune T cells. This transfer factor is made up of proteins from colostrum, the first milk provided by a mother cow for her new calf. The first milk contains valuable immune data meant to prepare the calf's vulnerable immune system for microbe attacks.

DHEA (dehydroepiandrosterone)

DHEA, an adrenal hormone, is the most abundant hormone in the body. It is often considered the mother hormone. DHEA is a precursor to the sex hormones as well as a number of other vital hormones in the body. Levels of DHEA are the highest when we are in the prime of life (ages twenty to thirty-five).

Benefits: Now available without prescription, DHEA has great value in preventing and treating osteoporosis, diabetes, cancer, Alzheimer's, cardiovascular disease, high cholesterol and other immune disorders, such as chronic fatigue syndrome and fibromyalgia. It is thought to be effective in reducing the symptoms of PMS and menopause, and believed to slow down and even reverse the aging process.

Glucosamine

Glucosamine is the key substance that determines how many proteoglycan (water-holding) molecules are formed in cartilage.

> *Benefits:* Very effective for improvement in arthritic conditions.

L-carnitine

L-carnitine is an amino acid that assists greatly in breaking down fats and sugars for energy in the metabolic process.

> *Benefits:* Effectively boosts energy levels in degenerative disease patients.

Magnesium

> *Benefits:* Essential part of the enzyme system and is most important in the rehabilitation of degenerative disease patients. Almost 100 percent of the victims I have worked with have exhibited a magnesium deficiency. Magnesium is involved in the absorption of potassium, calcium, phosphorus and B-complex vitamins, as well as vitamins C and E. Magnesium is also essential in ATP (energy) production.

Malic acid

> *Benefits:* An essential ingredient in the production of energy, it lessens the toxic effects of aluminum. When combined with magnesium, malic acid is very effective as a cleansing and healing agent for degenerative disease and other systemic conditions.

> *Sources:* Citrus fruits and apples.

Manganese

> *Benefits:* Essential for the proper and healthy functioning of the pituitary gland and the body's other glands. It is essential in the treatment of chronic

SUPPLEMENTS

disease because it aids glucose utilization for creating energy. It also helps the central nervous system function normally.

Melatonin

Benefits: Melatonin is a hormone that may affect common distresses such as sleep disorders, lack of immunity, aging and cancer. Melatonin is produced by the pineal gland, which is found in the center of the brain and releases melatonin when the eye is not receiving light. Melatonin contains vitamin E, one of the more powerful antioxidants and free-radical fighters.

Oil of oregano

Oil of oregano is derived from certain species of oregano plants. The medicinal oregano is different from the type usually found in the garden.

Benefits: Oil of oregano is the premier natural antiseptic with microbial killing powers. Every microbe against which it is tested succumbs to it. It is such an effective antiseptic that it cannot be matched either in the synthetic or natural arena in terms of its ability to kill a wide range of microbes.

Pycnogenol (proanthocyanidins)

Pycnogenol is produced from maritime pine bark. It has been determined by scientists to be fifty times stronger than vitamin E and twenty times stronger than vitamin C.

Benefits: It is a very powerful antioxidant that scavenges free radicals generated by foreign toxic chemicals. It helps to remove inflammation from the joints and other tissues and improves the nervous and immune systems. It strengthens collagen, improves circulation, enhances the permeability of cell walls, acts as a powerful antioxidant to boost the immune system, enhances metabolism and promotes healing in the body.

SUPPLEMENTS

Rice bran extract

Benefits: Rice bran extract contains a very potent form of vitamin E. Vitamin E is a powerful antioxidant, immune booster and detoxifier that helps with capillary wall strength, lung metabolism and muscle and nerve maintenance.

Selenium

Benefit: Selenium is an immune booster. It protects cells from the toxic effects of free radicals.

Sources: Shrimp, sunflower seeds, wheat breads, tuna and salmon.

Vitamin C

Vitamin C is one of the most powerful antioxidants that the body needs.

Sources: Fresh fruits such as grapefruit, strawberries, bananas, cantaloupe, papaya, kiwi, mango, raspberries, pineapple and tomatoes; vegetables such as cabbage, asparagus, broccoli, brussels sprouts, collard greens, potatoes and red peppers. Vitamin C is heat sensitive and easily destroyed by refining or overprocessing; therefore, foods containing vitamin C should be steamed or microwaved only for a very short period of time.

Vitamin E

Sources: Vegetable oils, especially safflower, avocados, nuts, sunflower seeds, wheat germ, whole-grain cereals and breads, asparagus, dried prunes and broccoli.

Zinc

Benefits: It helps with the absorption of vitamins in the body and helps form skin, nails and hair, as well as being an essential part of many enzymes involved in metabolism and digestion. Vitamin A must be present for zinc to be absorbed properly in the body.

SUPPLEMENTS

Sources: Some excellent sources of zinc are ginseng and the herb licorice.

These miracle nutrients can help to heal the most chronic forms of degenerative disease when included in a good nutritional plan along with the other elements of a healthy lifestyle as discussed in this book.

MUSCLE/CONNECTIVE TISSUE AND BIOFLAVONOIDS

I want to list a few more benefits of bioflavonoids for the degenerative disease sufferer. Bioflavonoids are found in virtually all plant foods and are essential for healthy capillary walls, the metabolism of vitamin C and for enhancing the utilization of other essential nutrients. There are literally thousands of different types of bioflavonoids. The bioflavonoids aid degenerative disease victims by:

- Enhancing the strength of collagen in connective tissue

- Strengthening muscle fiber

- Buffering free-radical damage and improving the functioning ability of muscle fiber

- Enhancing the energy production process

- Assisting in the utilization of other nutrients by the body

Some excellent sources of bioflavonoids are fresh fruits and vegetables, seeds, nuts, legumes, whole grains, citrus fruits, onions, berries, green tea and especially fruits that contain a pit (such as plums and cherries). There are also rose hip bioflavonoids as well as citrus bioflavonoids such as catechin, hesperidin, rutin, quercetin, milk thistle seed extract, ginkgo extracts, pycnogenol and rice bran extract.

SUPPLEMENTS

ANTIOXIDANTS: VITAL FOR YOUR HEALTH

A nutritional regimen is one of the key steps in safeguarding our health against chronic conditions. One of the most widely accepted theories is that disease and debilitation of the body are caused by unstable molecules called free radicals that rampage through the body, attacking healthy cells and destroying healthy tissue.

A free radical is a molecule that is missing an electron, which is caused by our breathing polluted air, metabolizing food substances in the body, consuming unhealthy food additives and so forth. These molecules that are missing electrons are not happy until they take a bite out of a healthy cell, damaging it and replacing the electron that is missing. Excessive and non-buffered free radicals are now thought to be the basic underlying cause of all diseases, including cancer, heart disease, diabetes, arthritis and degenerative diseases.

The good news is that antioxidants act as buffers between free radicals and good health. Antioxidants become the antidotes to the free radicals most commonly found in the body. They stabilize the free radicals, preventing them from attacking and damaging other body tissues.

We have listed the more powerful antioxidant vitamins: beta carotene, vitamin C, vitamin E and vitamin B_6. Some of the trace minerals that serve as powerful antioxidants are selenium, zinc, manganese, magnesium, boron and chromium. Some other powerful antioxidant and immune-boosting nutrients are coenzyme Q_{10}, pycnogenol, rice bran extract, curcumin and garlic.

SUPPLEMENTS

YES, SUPPLEMENTATION IS NECESSARY

As mentioned earlier, it is best to get vitamins, minerals, antioxidants and other nutrients the body needs from fresh whole foods (ideally organic foods) rather than supplements. However, proper amounts of vitamins, minerals and nutrients are very difficult to acquire from foods because of depleted soils and ingested chemicals in the form of pesticides and insecticides that interfere with proper nutrient absorption.

Is nutritional supplementation really necessary for healing and health? The answer is an unequivocal *yes*. In order to get all of the necessary nutrients in today's world, it is absolutely essential that we take supplements, especially when treating chronic conditions.

If by virtue of your personal analysis, after having read the first half of this book, you find yourself confirming one or several of the symptoms or characteristics relating to chronic fatigue, degenerative disease or other systemic conditions, then you are in dire need of my rebuilding/rebalancing program. And if you are susceptible to colds, flu, viruses or general tiredness, you are a prime candidate for a supplementation program.

In that case, you are probably, like most people, eating a good amount of sugar, high-fat foods and packaged processed foods with harmful additives and fillers. Your exercise habits, daily diet, normal routine and self-esteem are probably not what they should be. This is the typical routine that gradually, over the years, leads you to become unbalanced and unhealthy. It's very likely that you are basically unhappy and possibly view the world as a depressing place.

Most people falling into this category will almost always exhibit one or more of the debilitating symptoms of being out of balance. This downward spiraling effect must be reversed, or the immune system will eventually become weakened and overwhelmed to the point that it can no longer protect the body so that it can renew and heal itself. Those experiencing the declining health status described above very often will have carried some of the unhealthy symptoms for many years, seen a number of doctors and accumulated an extensive medical record in search of a cure for their ongoing physical and emotional problems.

As you commit to improving your nutritional regimen and adding the necessary supplementation of vitamins, minerals and miracle nutrients to your diet, you will begin to feel better and have a new outlook on life. This new perspective will help you to add the next vital step of your rehabilitation to health: exercise. Even if you are in pain and the prospect of moving your body makes you groan, please read the next chapter and begin to find the freedom that the power of exercise offers you.

SUPPLEMENTS

CHAPTER 8

Step 5:
The Power of Exercise

Get Moving

> **But those who wait on the Lᴏʀᴅ shall renew their strength; they shall mount up with wings like eagles, they shall run and not be weary, they shall walk and not faint.**
>
> **—Iꜱᴀɪᴀʜ 40:31**

You may have heard many times that exercise is absolutely vital for your health. There is monumental evidence that exercise will lower cancer risk, lower blood pressure and cholesterol, remedy sleep problems, take off unwanted weight and reduce the risk of heart disease. Without the benefit of exercise on a regular basis, bones become brittle and muscles atrophy and become weaker. When the skin of athletes is examined under a microscope, it is validated that they have thicker, healthier skin with stronger collagen than people who do not exercise.

When the prophet Isaiah promised us that we could mount up with wings as eagles, he was obviously using the analogy to refer to spiritual strength and exploits, but it is interesting that he used the picture of physical fitness—running without fatigue and walking without weakness. As we learn to seek God for His pathway to health, we will learn how to overcome mental and spiritual difficulties, as well as

EXERCISE

111

physical ones, that will allow us to soar like the eagle through life.

Unfortunately, a large percentage of people avoid exercise, considering it a time-consuming, rigorous, painful chore. This really does not have to be the case. My Body Advantage Exercise System is designed for fun, convenience and simplicity. It requires only a commitment to do what it takes to recover good health. With this healthy perspective, you will begin to enjoy the movement and the achievement of your exercise goals.

I receive phone calls on a regular basis from around the world that begin, "Dr. Elrod, I am reading your book and have begun your program. It has given me new hope about getting my life back from the chronic fatigue I have suffered for years." I can tell you that nothing will contribute more to fatigue, a weakened immune system and general poor health than a lifestyle without regular exercise along with poor nutrition.

These happy callers tell me that after only a few days of beginning The Body Advantage Program, eating adequate fruits, veggies, complex carbohydrates, quality protein and healthy fats, they have much more energy, are less sluggish and begin to sleep better. I have experienced these joyful testimonies dozens of times with patients around the world.

I rejoice with them, and I remind them that for complete recovery and long-lasting health, it is critical to add the step of exercise.

THE HEALING NATURE
OF EXERCISE

If you suffer with a degenerative disease, you probably already know that exercise is necessary for the muscles and joints. But you also know that exercise can feel very painful for those with health problems. Our bodies have been designed to perform an incredible array of activities. In normal circumstances, our muscles and joints are in constant motion, but when we are ill or injured, we have a natural tendency to slow down and stop our normal activities in favor of rest and recovery.

The right balance of exercise has an extremely powerful, positive detoxification effect on the cells of the body—one of the keys to health and vitality.

EXERCISE

When we are inactive, our unused muscles and bones start to atrophy, or waste away. As a result, the symptoms of degenerative disease progress more rapidly. As we have already learned in the previous chapters, it is important to treat degenerative disease with good nutrition and supplements. It is just as important to continue exercising in order to keep the muscles healthy and flexible. Exercise buffers the debilitating effects of degenerative symptoms in the following important ways:

- It strengthens ligaments and tendons while enhancing muscle tone.

- It increases flexibility or stretch-ability of muscle tissue.

- It increases circulation and the flow of oxygen and nutrients to muscle fibers.

- It increases healing, pain-relieving power endorphins.

- It boosts the immune system.

- It enhances levels of serotonin and growth hormone.

- It increases synovial fluid into and out of the cartilage in the joints.

To enjoy optimal health, you must become convinced that exercise is one of the more beneficial steps to health and healing.

THE EXERCISE PROGRAM PROTOCOL

I personally believe that three major areas of exercise—stretching, cardiovascular and muscle-strengthening exercises—can be performed safely and effectively by most people who suffer from systemic conditions. I want to give you some guidelines to help you develop an exercise program that will combine with good nutrition to alleviate your degenerative disease distress.

As you develop an exercise program, remember that common sense and moderation are always the rule when beginning an exercise program. Contact your physician for a thorough examination.

Don't waste your time with a personal trainer who is not familiar with your condition and is not trained to design programs for people

EXERCISE

with physical limitations. It is vitally important that you seek the advice of a professional exercise specialist to assist you in designing an exercise program. These specialists can generally be found at your local health clubs, YMCAs and fitness centers.

Your exercise program will be designed to build up muscle and intensity gradually. Your program should include cardiovascular fitness, muscular strength and muscular flexibility.

Keep these guidelines in mind as you proceed with your program:

- Begin slowly. Don't push yourself to the point of injury.

- Recognize the difference between slight muscle soreness as a result of your workout and aggravation of chronic pain.

- If you feel dizzy, become nauseated, short of breath or feel pain in your chest, stop exercising immediately.

- Increase your intensity (how hard you exercise) gradually, giving your body time to adapt.

- Warm up properly to avoid unnecessary injury.

- Cool down gradually to bring the heart rate and body temperature down slowly.

The human body was created to be a very physical, active, moving mechanism. When we stay active, the body stays strong, fit and efficient. When we don't, our quality of life is compromised significantly by weight gain, increase in body fat, loss of muscle mass and loss of bone density. Inactivity may also lead to one of the many hypo-kinetic or systemic diseases ranging from headache and sleep disruption to lupus, fibromyalgia, cancer or heart disease. So, in addition to taking the stairs and turning off the television, it's time to put on your workout duds and learn how to exercise properly, if you haven't already.

EXERCISE

Remember to get clearance from your physician before beginning any exercise program.

STRETCHING EXERCISES

Many people who suffer from degenerative diseases adopt more sedentary living habits and become more inactive than normal because of the pain and lack of energy that are usually associated with their condition. This inactivity causes decreased flexibility. Stretching is very important for those who suffer from these painful conditions.

The most common areas where people lose flexibility is in the front of the hip, the back of the thigh, the lower back and the neck and shoulders. There are basic flexibility exercises for the large muscle groups in these areas. There can be tremendous benefits for incorporating proper stretching exercises into your lifestyle. However, unless these exercises are done properly, they can do more harm than good and possibly even cause damage.

Guidelines for maximum benefit from your flexibility program

- Choose a comfortable stretching routine using a mat or The Body Advantage Exercise System.

- Do light calisthenics or walk for three to five minutes to increase blood flow and body temperature before stretching.

- Be sure to stretch all major muscle groups (arms and shoulders, lower back, legs).

- Stretch gently, bending joints slightly if necessary in the beginning.

- Avoid bouncing to prevent muscle tear and joint damage.

- Stretch three to five times a week on a regular basis; always stretch before aerobic or strength training.

- Always stretch after exercising. This eliminates lactic acid, which prevents soreness.

Muscle flexibility

Muscle inflexibility can cause excessive stress and force to be exerted on areas of the body opposite the movement. This can very easily lead to injury and cause further problems. All types of movement—aerobic activities as well as strength development

EXERCISE

activities—can improve flexibility.

The more effective and efficient flexibility exercises utilize stretch devices such as elastic tubing. The elastic tubing devices are especially effective because generally they allow you to include both strength development and flexibility movement. Exercise at a gym or at home using The Body Advantage Exercise System.

THE BODY ADVANTAGE BASIC STRETCH ROUTINE

Reverse Shoulder Stretch
(Muscles developed: arms, shoulders, calf)

1. Anchor tubing at shoulder level, with back to anchor.

2. Hold handles over top of shoulders, palms facing inward, elbows bent with forearms parallel to floor.

3. Move away from door until tubing is taut.

4. Stride forward with one foot in front of the other, knee bent on front leg, with back leg remaining straight and heel of rear foot remaining on floor to insure a good stretch on calf of back leg.

5. Keep spine straight, pushing head and chest forward, allowing arms and shoulders to be pulled toward anchor.

6. Hold for a count of 4 (1001, 1002, etc.)

7. Repeat above with the opposite foot forward.

8. Complete two reps with each foot.

EXERCISE

Reverse Shoulder and Chest Stretch
(Muscles developed: chest, upper back, shoulders)

1. Anchor tubing at shoulder level, back to anchor.
2. Hold handles directly behind back, palms facing outward, arms parallel to floor.
3. Move away from door until tubing is taut.
4. Stride forward with one foot in front of the other; bend knee of forward leg, with back leg remaining straight and heel of rear foot remaining on floor to insure a good stretch on calf of back leg.
5. Keep spine straight, pushing head and chest forward, allowing arms and shoulders to be pulled toward anchor and allowing hands to be pulled together.
6. Hold for a count of 4 (1001, 1002, etc.)
7. Repeat above with the opposite foot forward.
8. Complete two reps with each foot.

EXERCISE

Lower Back and Hamstring Stretch
(Muscles developed: lower back, buttocks,
hamstrings, arms, shoulders)

1. Anchor tubing at top of door, with back to anchor.

2. Hold handles over top of shoulders, palms facing inward, elbows bent with forearms parallel to floor.

3. Stand erect 12–18 inches from door, feet shoulder width.

4. Bend forward at the waist slowly, knees slightly bent; continue moving the head toward the floor until you reach a maximum, comfortable stretch—DO NOT BOUNCE, and do not overstretch.

5. Hold for a count of 4 (1001, 1002, etc.)

6. Return slowly to a standing erect position.

7. Complete four reps.

8. As blood flow and muscle temperature increases, the stretch can be comfortably increased with each rep.

EXERCISE

Lower Back and Quadriceps Stretch
(Muscles developed: lower back, buttocks,
quadriceps, arms, shoulders)

1. Anchor tubing at top of door, with back to anchor.

2. Hold handles over top of shoulders, palms facing inward, elbows bent with forearms parallel to floor.

3. Stand erect 12–18 inches from door, feet shoulder width.

4. Leaning slightly forward, bend knees and lower weight slowly until sitting on heels; raise heels off floor with weight balanced on balls of feet and toes. Holding handles for balance, bend lower back for a good stretch while looking at floor.

5. Hold for a count of 4 (1001, 1002, etc.)

6. Complete a second rep after returning to a standing erect position.

EXERCISE

STRENGTH AND TONING

Muscle tone and strength will help to prevent unnecessary injuries that occur during normal daily activities. Perhaps you have been injured while playing ball in the yard or putting a box on a closet shelf. The lack of muscular strength may be the culprit. Strength training, also called resistance training, involves repeatedly lifting a weight or moving against a resistance. Examples of resistance exercises include lifting free weights like dumbbells or barbells and using weight machines and resistance devices like elastic tubing.

Be sure that you do not begin your strength training too vigorously. It is important to get started at an appropriate, comfortable level and progress gradually. Depending upon the severity of your condition, you may need to start with three- to five-pound weights or an equivalent resistance with an elastic tubing device. I would strongly recommend beginning your exercises with dumbbells (small weights that can be held in one hand), weight machines or elastic tubing devices. These are much easier to work with and much safer than the larger, heavier free weights.

- Begin with light weights with which you can do ten repetitions (reps).

- One set of ten reps is enough for muscle toning and strength.

- Progress gradually by increasing weight as desired.

- Stagger your days, exercising, for example, Monday, Wednesday and Friday.

EXERCISE

THE BODY ADVANTAGE BASIC STRENGTH ROUTINE

Bicep Curl
(Muscles developed: biceps, shoulders [front])

1. Securely place tubing under feet.
2. Arms down by sides, palms forward, elbows anchored at waist, knees and waist slightly flexed (bent).
3. Curl hands slowly to shoulders; return slowly to sides.
4. Do eight to twelve reps (increase reps as desired with progress).

EXERCISE

Chest Press
(Muscles developed: upper arms, chest, shoulders)

1. Anchor tubing at shoulder level, back to anchor.
2. Feet shoulder width apart, knees bent, trunk forward with back straight, hands in front of shoulders with elbows pointing back.
3. Push hands straight forward, slowly straightening arms, and return slowly to starting position.
4. Do eight to twelve reps (increase reps as desired with progress).

Posterior Shoulder Row
(Muscles developed: arms, shoulders, rear upper back)

1. Anchor tubing at shoulder level.
2. Feet shoulder width apart, knees bent, trunk forward with

EXERCISE

back straight, arms straight, reaching toward the anchor with palms in.

3. Pull hands to chest, keeping elbows near sides, then return slowly to starting position.

4. Do eight to twelve reps (increase reps as desired with progress).

Triceps Pull
(Muscles developed: triceps [back of arms], upper back)

1. Anchor tubing at shoulder level.

2. Stand with feet shoulder width apart, knees slightly bent. Drop buttocks straight down with trunk bent forward slightly, spine straight, keeping the weight slightly in front of the feet.

3. Stand with back to door, tubing taut, hands in front of shoulders with upper arms parallel to floor.

4. Push hands forward parallel to floor until arms are straightened; return hands to starting position with a steady deliberate movement, maintaining resistance as the hands move back toward the shoulder.

5. Do eight to twelve reps (increase reps as desired with progress).

EXERCISE

Lateral Pull
(Muscles developed: arms, laterals)

1. Anchor tubing at top of door or at an overhead connection.
2. Stand facing the anchor with arms outstretched forward at shoulder level, tubing taut, palms facing down.
3. Bend knees, trunk leaning forward with buttock over heels.
4. Pull hands down until even with outside of thighs.
5. Allow hands to steadily return to the starting position while maintaining control and resistance on the return.
6. Do eight to twelve reps (increase reps as desired with progress).

EXERCISE

Reverse Lunge
(Muscles developed: quadriceps, buttocks, lower back)

1. Anchor tubing at top of door.

2. Facing anchor, back away until tubing is taut for balance; stand erect, then bring one leg up in front with knee bent, balancing on opposite foot.

3. Bring leg down and reach back as far as possible, planting toe firmly on floor. Front thigh should be parallel to floor.

4. Return to starting position with tension constantly on the forward leg.

5. Do eight to twelve reps, then repeat with opposite leg. (Increase reps as desired with progress.)

EXERCISE

Side Shoulder Raise
(Muscles developed: upper back, shoulders,
middle upper back)

1. Securely place the tubing under feet.

2. Ready position: spine straight, waist slightly bent with trunk forward.

3. Starting position is with hands at side, palms facing inward, elbows slightly bent.

4. Slowly pull the arms away from sides, raising hands as high as possible, keeping arms straight with only a slight bend at the elbows.

5. Return slowly to starting position; without relaxing, begin next rep.

6. Do eight to twelve reps (increase reps as desired with progress).

EXERCISE

Abdominal Crunch
(Muscles developed: abdominals, quadriceps, buttocks)

1. Anchor tubing at lower setting (ankle level).

2. Lie on back with head nearest anchor; hold handles with arms outstretched and feet 6 inches off floor, tubing taut for resistance.

3. Keeping legs straight with feet raised, curl head and shoulders off floor while simultaneously bending knees to meet elbows.

4. Return slowly to starting position, not allowing feet to touch floor until all reps are completed.

5. Do eight to twelve reps (increase reps as desired with progress).

EXERCISE

Inner Thigh Pull
(Muscles developed: inner thigh, buttocks)

1. Anchor tubing at lower setting (ankle level).

2. Place one handle through the other and draw tubing away from door until taut.

3. Place right foot into handle at ankle level, with right side toward door and feet spread with left foot slightly behind right foot, balancing using chair back, desk, etc.

4. Move away from door until right leg is outstretched to the door away from midline.

5. Move foot slowly from right to left until foot crosses body's midline as far as possible. Pause for 1 second, then allow foot to move slowly back to the starting position using inner thigh muscles. This insures maximum results while moving foot away from door as well as back toward door.

6. Do eight to twelve reps. (Increase reps and/or distance from the anchor as desired with progress.)

EXERCISE

Body Twist
(Muscles developed: trunk rotators, shoulder, chest)

1. Anchor tubing in middle position (shoulder level).

2. Place one handle through the other and pull single handle away from anchor until tubing is taut.

3. Stand with right side to anchor and right arm outstretched pointing to anchor. Feet should be shoulder width apart. Twist body to left as far as possible, pulling tubing tight around the right shoulder. Hold for one second, then return to starting position.

4. Do eight to twelve reps, then repeat same movement with left arm from opposite side. Increase number of reps and distance from anchor as desired with progress.

EXERCISE

SPORTS SKILLS

Tennis

Golf

Archer's Bow

All Sports

EXCELLENT AEROBIC EXERCISE CHOICES

There are many excellent aerobic exercises you can choose for your exercise program. Most health clubs and YMCAs have a wide array of aerobic classes and activities from which to choose once you are through Phase I and are ready to accelerate your program. Here is some information about some of the favorite aerobic exercises:

Walking

Almost anyone—including sufferers of chronic pain and disease—can include walking as a complete, convenient, effective and enjoyable way to lose weight and restore or maintain total health. Walking has many benefits.

- It burns calories and fat.
- It tones and strengthens muscles.
- It boosts energy.
- It improves total health and well-being.
- It improves muscle flexibility.
- It eliminates early morning stiffness.
- It alleviates muscle pain.
- It improves overall muscle physiology.
- It brightens the outlook on life, lifting the spirit.

For best results, you should be performing within your target heart rate zone, which is somewhere between 50 percent and 70 percent of your maximum heart rate. The maximum heart rate is calculated as

EXERCISE

maximum potential of the human heart at birth (220 beats per minute for maximum exertion for work or exercise). We potentially lose one heartbeat capacity per year as we age—thus the equation to subtract your age from 220. To compute the lower range of your target heart rate (THR), subtract your age from 220, and then subtract your resting heart rate (RHR), multiply by .5, and then add your resting heart rate back into the figure. Then follow the same formula, but multiply by .7 to get the upper range for your THR. The numeric formula is as follows:

(220 - Your Age - RHR (resting heart rate)) x 0.5 + RHR = THR

For example, for a forty-year-old with a resting heart rate of 65, the equation would look like this:

- $(220 - 40 - 65) \times 0.5 + 65 = 123$
- $(220 - 40 - 65) \times 0.7 + 65 = 146$

Aquatics

Swimming and water exercises are very helpful to many chronic conditions, and you can avoid the joint strain that sometimes occurs with other types of exercise. Water therapy can be most beneficial, especially in heated pools. Water exercises can be performed in shallow water or with flotation devices, and do not require that the participant have any swimming experience. Some of the benefits of aquatic activities and exercises include:

- Provides stability and support, especially beneficial for advanced conditions
- Relieves stress and anxiety
- Promotes muscle relaxation, therefore enhancing relief of pain
- Develops stronger, more flexible muscles
- Provides low-impact exercise for the joints
- Promotes social interaction
- Boosts confidence
- Improves heart health and lung capacity
- Increases serotonin and growth hormone levels
- Stimulates production of T cells and strengthens the immune system

EXERCISE

Cycling

If you suffer from a great deal of pain around the knees and in the hip joints, cycling could be an excellent alternative. There are many benefits to cycling, including:

- Takes weight off the legs and hips
- Relieves lower back pain
- Conditions the heart and lungs
- Strengthens the quadriceps (thigh muscles) more than walking
- Strengthens the muscles around the knee joints

PHYSICAL ACTIVITY CALORIE USE CHART

This chart shows the approximate calories spent per hour by a 100-, 150- and 200-pound person for the following activities:[1]

Activity	100-pound person	150-pound person	200-pound person
Bicycling, 6 mph	160	240	312
Bicycling, 12 mph	270	410	534
Jogging, 7 mph	610	920	1,230
Jumping rope	500	750	1,000
Running, 5.5 mph	440	660	962
Running, 10 mph	850	1,280	1,664
Swimming, 25 yds/min	185	275	358
Swimming, 50 yds/min	325	500	650
Tennis singles	265	400	535
Walking, 2 mph	160	240	312
Walking, 3 mph	210	320	416
Walking, 4.5 mph	295	440	572

EXERCISE

INCREASE PHYSICAL ACTIVITY IN YOUR DAILY LIFE

There are simple changes you can make during your normal routine that will improve your level of physical activity and improve your health. The following recommendations for increasing activity at home, at the office and at play are a combination of my study and that of the American Heart Association.

At home

There are advantages to working out at home: It's convenient, comfortable and safe. Working out at home also allows your children to see you being active, which sets a good example for them. You can combine exercise with other activities, such as watching TV. If you buy exercise equipment, it's a one-time expense and can be used by other members of the family. And it's easy to have short bouts of activity several times a day. Here are some recommendations:

- Do housework yourself instead of hiring someone else to do it.

- Work in the garden or mow the grass. Using a riding mower doesn't count! Rake leaves, prune, dig and pick up trash.

- Go out for a short walk before breakfast, after dinner or both! Start with five to ten minutes, and work up to thirty minutes.

- Walk or bike to the corner store instead of driving.

- When walking, pick up the pace from leisurely to brisk. Choose a hilly route.

- When watching TV, sit up instead of lying on the sofa. Better yet, spend a few minutes pedaling on your stationary bicycle while watching TV. Throw away your video remote control. Instead of asking someone to bring you a drink, get off your chair and get it yourself.

- Stand up while talking on the telephone.

- Walk the dog, whether you have one or not (smile).

- Save money—wash your own car, and give the car wash a rest.

- Park farther away at the shopping mall and walk the extra distance. Wear your walking shoes and

EXERCISE

sneak in an extra lap or two around the mall.

- At the grocery store push the cart up and down every aisle, and make a final lap around the store before leaving.

- Stretch to reach items in high places, and squat or bend to look at items at floor level.

- Save money—chop and split your own wood (warm yourself twice).

- Vacuum your home frequently.

- Keep exercise equipment repaired—and use it!

- Walk to the mailbox instead of driving (i.e., apartment complex mail centers).

- Do stretches before and after bathing or showering.

- Mind-set: Frequently climb in-home stairs rather than avoiding them.

- When you shovel your driveway, do a good deed and shovel your neighbor's driveway as well.

At the office

Most of us have sedentary jobs. Work takes up a significant part of the day. What can you do to increase your physical activity during the workday? Here are some recommendations:

- Take The Body Advantage Exercise System with you to work and do stretching and toning exercises during breaks or lunch. (See product page to order.)

- Take The Body Advantage Exercise System with you when you travel and do stretching and toning exercises in your hotel room.

- Brainstorm project ideas with a coworker while taking a walk.

- Stand while talking on the telephone.

- Walk down the hall to speak with someone rather than using the telephone.

EXERCISE

- Take the stairs instead of the elevator. Or get off a few floors early and take the stairs the rest of the way.

- Walk to your gate instead of riding trams and escalators at the airport.

- Walk around the terminal and window-shop rather than sitting while waiting for the plane. (Choose water for your airport drinks rather than the bar.)

- When permitted, walk up and down the aisle in the airplane, train or bus.

- Stay at hotels with fitness centers or swimming pools—and use them—while on business trips.

- Take along a jump rope in your suitcase when you travel. Jump and do calisthenics in your hotel room.

- Participate in or start a recreation league at your company.

- Form a sports team to raise money for charity events.

- Join a fitness center or Y near your work. Work out before or after work to avoid rush-hour traffic, or drop by for a noon workout.

- Schedule exercise time on your business calendar, and treat it as any other important appointment.

- Get off the bus a few blocks early and walk the rest of the way to work or home.

- Walk around your building for a break during the workday or during lunch.

EXERCISE

At play

Play and recreation are important for good health. Look for opportunities to be active and have fun at the same time. Here are some suggestions:

- Plan family outings and vacations that include

physical activity (for example, hiking, back-packing or swimming).

- See the sights in new cities by walking, jogging or bicycling.

- Make a date with a friend to enjoy your favorite physical activities. Do them regularly.

- Listen to your favorite music, something that motivates you, while exercising.

- Dance with someone or by yourself. Take dancing lessons. Hit the dance floor on fast numbers instead of slow ones.

- Join a recreational club that emphasizes physical activity.

- At the beach, sit and watch the waves instead of lying flat. Better yet, get up and walk, run or fly a kite.

- When golfing, walk instead of using a cart.

- Play singles tennis or racquetball instead of doubles.

- At a picnic, join in on badminton instead of croquet.

- At the lake, rent a rowboat instead of a canoe.

MY EXERCISE PLAN

It will be helpful for you to begin to think of ways you can increase your exercise in activities you enjoy and are possible for your present health condition. I recommend you do the following:

EXERCISE

1. List ways you will increase physical activity:

   _____

   _____

   _____

   _____

   _____

2. List favorite aerobic activities:

   _____

   _____

   _____

   _____

   _____

3. List aerobic and strength activities you would like
   to learn:

   _____

   _____

   _____

   _____

   _____

EXERCISE

CHAPTER 9

Step 6:
Restoring Deep Sleep

Establishing Restful Healing

> **I will both lie down in peace, and sleep; for You alone, O LORD, make me dwell in safety.**
> **—PSALM 4:8**

The final crucial step to our model for restoring health and returning to an active, vibrant lifestyle is restful sleep. Most people who suffer from degenerative disease do not get enough rest, even if they sleep eight hours. Sleep disorders are often devastating symptoms of chronic disease. Sleep may be almost impossible because of pain in the muscles and connective tissues

In order for the body to rebuild itself and defend against chronic fatigue, stress and depression, you must regularly experience deep sleep, known as level 4 sleep. A lack of this restful sleep weakens your immune system, making you more susceptible to chronic illnesses.

ESTABLISHING RESTFUL HEALING

Your potential for restoring deep, replenishing sleep will be helped greatly by the following suggestions.

RESTORING SLEEP

Eliminate or restrict caffeine and alcohol consumption.

These harmful substances can especially affect your sleep if you ingest them during the afternoon and evening hours. Having a nightcap before going to bed may feel like it is helping initially, but it will actually leave you tired and listless the next morning.

Eat healthfully and supplement with vitamins.

Following just a few of the simple nutritional guidelines we have discussed, such as lowering saturated fat, limiting fried foods, increasing fiber and limiting sugar intake, will enhance better sleep. Also, eating more fruits and vegetables, along with taking a healthy regimen of vitamins and minerals, has a cleansing and balancing effect on the body that works to promote better sleep.

Establish a structure for healing.

For most people, it helps to develop a routine of retiring and rising at about the same time on a daily basis. It can be devastating for the chronic illness sufferer to retire later than normal, causing him or her to lose a good night's sleep. Some of the symptoms may return almost immediately with such a disruption. It is also a good idea to have meals on a regular schedule as well to avoid stressing the body during its recovery.

Manage stress.

Deep breathing and muscle relaxation exercises are very helpful, even for a few minutes several times a day, to relieve stress. Stretching for a few minutes throughout the day can also alleviate the effects of stress in your body and mind. These simple movements will increase blood flow, energizing you to complete the tasks ahead. I have included a few helpful exercises in this book, but don't be afraid to do some research on your own to find the exercises or activities that will work best for you. Anything that relieves stress can be added to your routine.

Relax.

Recreation involves different activities for different kinds of people. Whatever you enjoy doing to relax should be given priority in your life. Playing with your dog or going to a movie—just having fun—are inexpensive therapies that will reward you with a positive outlook and renewed energy.

RESTORING SLEEP

Exercise regularly.

Exercise is a very effective way to eliminate the effects of stress. It is essential for reducing tension. If chronic pain has caused you to become more and more sedentary and inactive, resulting in muscle and joint atrophy and pain, exercise will strengthen and restore flexibility to your muscles, eventually reducing and eliminating the pain associated with chronic illness. It also stimulates the production of growth hormone needed for healthy muscle and soft tissue. The combined effects of exercise will also help you sleep better—as long as you do not exercise too late in the day. Late exercise could disrupt your sleep.

Wind down.

Find a comfortable way to quiet your body and mind, and consider the happy and positive aspects of your life as you wind down from the activities of the day. Perhaps a warm bath or reading a good book can serve as an enjoyable way to wind down from the busyness of your day. Establishing a nightly routine will help prepare your body and mind for the restful sleep you need to renew your strength. And it will help to relieve the effects of the day's stresses.

Create a comfortable sleep environment.

Exposure to light controls our wakefulness and sleeping, which is regulated by circadian rhythms in a twenty-four-hour cycle. The secretion of hormones, particularly melatonin, is also a part of this fascinating cycle. Because darkness helps to stimulate these hormones, it is important to block out light from your bedroom, perhaps by utilizing heavy curtains or shades. You may also choose to use music, white noise or recorded nature sounds (such as waves or waterfalls) to block outside distracting noises. It is also helpful to refrain from doing study, work or other daytime activities in your bedroom.

SPIRITUAL KEY TO RESTFUL SLEEP

We can never ignore the mind-body connection or the spiritual realities that govern them. God ordained that our bodies would need restful sleep for health, and He created us to rest in the darkness of each night. He also gave instructions about our week:

> Work shall be done for six days, but the seventh day shall
> be a holy day for you, a Sabbath of rest to the LORD.
> *—Exodus 35:2*

RESTORING SLEEP

While our American lifestyle influences us more and more to ignore the Sabbath day, we were created with the need to keep a day of rest each week. The rhythm of this weekly cycle should be maintained in order to ensure health. It is helpful to take time to reflect and meditate on God, attend worship services, enjoy quiet recreation with family and friends, and just have some downtime from making a living.

We have included a few of the promises of God's Word regarding His desire for our health and healing. His desire for us is good, and He keeps His promises to those who qualify by seeking Him. The Scriptures declare:

> Blessed be the LORD, who has given rest to His people Israel, according to all that He promised. There has not failed one word of all His good promise, which He promised through His servant Moses.
>
> *—1 Kings 8:56*

Our Lord Himself encouraged us to find rest in Him when He said:

> Come to Me, all you who labor and are heavy laden, and I will give you rest. Take My yoke upon you and learn from Me, for I am gentle and lowly in heart, and you will find rest for your souls.
>
> *—Matthew 11:28–29*

As you commit to making lifestyle changes that will restore health to your body, don't forget the importance of relieving your mind and spirit of its stress by making peace with God and receiving His promises for life and health. This is extremely calming and relaxing, and it adds significantly to the ability to return to restful, restorative sleep.

WAYS TO IMPROVE SLEEP

- Take time to play.
- Reduce caffeine and alcohol.
- Wind down before retiring.
- Establish a regular sleep schedule.

RESTORING SLEEP

- Do not do any work, study or daytime activities in the bedroom.

- Don't watch TV in the bedroom.

- Use white noise (such as forest/beach sounds).

- Use a quality mattress and pillow.

- Kick the pets out of the bedroom.

- Block out light.

- Turn off or remove the telephone from the bedroom.

Note: See chapter seven, "Supplement for Efficiency," for calming vitamins, minerals and herbs as well as more information on relaxation and sleep.

PART III

*Special Help for
Your Condition*

CHAPTER 10

Protocol for Specific Systemic Conditions

Pathway to Overcoming Degenerative Disease

> **But the path of the just is like the shining sun,
> that shines ever brighter unto the perfect day.**
> —Proverbs 4:18

Acute diseases have a rapid onset and last a relatively short term with discomfort and distress, contrary to chronic and long-term degenerative disease, which, by virtue of its name, reveals an unending syndrome.

Acute disease is actually a built-in safety valve to cleanse and purify the body. Henry Lindlahr, M.D. of the early 1900s called acute diseases a cure within themselves. The body cleanses itself and eradicates toxins through influenza, diarrhea, boils, appendicitis, bladder infections, jaundice, gout, gastritis, smallpox, colds, virus and fever. On the other hand, chronic, degenerative disease starts slowly and persists over long periods, sometimes for a lifetime.

TREATING CHRONIC CONDITIONS

For the treatment of these chronic conditions, I recommend the use of natural remedies as an alternative treatment approach instead of conventional application of drugs. Because chronic conditions persist over time, they can require a continued use of drugs, which will eventually compromise the immune system. The body then becomes more vulnerable, and the patient can begin to suffer from a myriad of conditions as opposed to just one chronic or degenerative disease. Evaluate the following key areas concerning your daily nutritional intake.

Limit caffeine, sugar and fiber.

Excessive caffeine and sugar in the diet will rob the body of calcium. The popularity of coffee shops in America is contributing heavily to this health problem. If you consume a lot of fiber in your diet, take calcium between meals or at night before going to bed. This will help keep fiber from binding calcium and preventing its absorption. In fact, before bedtime is an excellent time to take calcium as it is also a wonderful sleep aid, having a calming influence on the body.

Minimize protein.

The more protein you have in your diet, the more calcium is eliminated from your body. The body requires only about 10 to 20 percent of the total diet to be protein. The popular high-protein diets in America are contributing significantly to the problem of osteoporosis.

Keep the pH balanced.

The American diet is highly acidic, filled with excessive meats, sugars, starches, coffee, soft drinks and simple carbohydrates. This high-protein, highly acidic diet keeps the body in a constant vulnerable state for osteoporosis. The pH of foods actually determines the level of acidity or alkalinity of fluids in the body (blood, saliva, urine).

If a body remains acidic over a period of time, this acidic condition will destroy the bones because the body will extract calcium and other minerals from them to use in buffering acids and attempting to balance the pH. The ideal pH of the urine should be between 6.5 and 7.0. If the pH is less than 6, acidosis has occurred. The majority of people in America are acidic, a major contributing factor to the degenerative disease dilemma. This is no mystery since America feasts on acid-producing foods such as fats, sugar, coffee, breads, meats, potatoes and pasta. Fruits and vegetables are alkaline-producing foods, the keys to good health nutritionally. Remember, God's greatest desire is that you receive wisdom so that you may enjoy His divine peace and health.

As I mentioned, about 50 percent of your diet should be fresh fruits and vegetables to help insure a higher body alkalinity with a balanced pH. You may wonder how the acidity of citrus fruits can contribute to alkalinity of the body. The fact is that while grapefruit, lemons, limes, oranges and many types of berries are acidic outside the body, they are alkalinizing once inside the body. God gave us alkaline bodies and specific instructions for eating in order to keep them alkaline, healthy and disease free. Early in the history of man, He instructed him in this regard:

> And God said, "See, I have given you every herb that yields seed which is on the face of all the earth, and every tree whose fruit yields seed; to you it shall be for food."
> —*Genesis 1:29*

An acidic body can be compared to a stagnant pond with no fresh water inlet or outlet. This acidic state allows fungus and harmful bacteria to flourish in your body. On the contrary, harmful bacteria, fungi, cancer cells and so forth cannot exist and thrive in an alkaline body with a strong immune system. That is why it is so important to eat healthfully, exercise and take helpful supplements to assist in keeping the pH balanced and the body in a healthy, alkaline state.

If a body remains acidic, this acidic condition will destroy the bones.

Lemon in your water

Add fresh lemon juice to your distilled water. Always order fresh-cut lemon when in restaurants, and add fresh lemon to your 20-ounce bottles of water throughout the day. Fresh lemon is a very powerful antioxidant and is high in vitamin C, which is also needed for the absorption of calcium and for defeating osteoporosis.

Green food

The green grasses and seaweeds are in the "super food" category because of their power to help keep the body alkaline with a balanced pH. Cucumber and aloe vera are excellent, especially when combined together in a synergistic formula. I recommend a super green drink that includes wheat grass, barley grass, spirulina, chlorella (chlorophyll), blue-green algae and flaxseed. Chlorella has a cracked shell and is effective for absorbing the toxic heavy metals out of the system. One of our health hazards is our excessive exposure to aluminum, lead, mercury and other metals that become toxic to the body in excess.

Spiritual assistance

Let me remind you to go to God's Word for additional help. He has promised to be there for you in times of need, especially when you are faced with trials and tribulation. If you have been diagnosed with osteoporosis, for example, you have a need for strength, energy and discipline to overcome this physical challenge and return to health and vitality. Take courage from promises like these:

> You whom I have taken from the ends of the earth, and called from its farthest regions, and said to you, "You are My servant, I have chosen you and have not cast you away: Fear not, for I am with you; be not dismayed, for I am your God. I will strengthen you, yes, I will help you, I will uphold you with My righteous right hand."
>
> —*Isaiah 41:9–10*

> But those who wait on the LORD shall renew their strength; they shall mount up with wings like eagles, they shall run and not be weary, they shall walk and not faint.
>
> —*Isaiah 40:31*

After presenting my complete protocol for reversing degenerative, chronic conditions in the first sections of this book and recommending several nutritional considerations above, I have now selected a few common systemic conditions to give you a brief outline of natural, alternative approaches for treatment. I am convinced that when you begin to commit to the entire protocol along with these specific suggestions, you will experience relief as you consistently apply the principles for health that we have discussed. Literally hundreds of people have experienced relief and recovery from their degenerative and systemic conditions after using my protocol.

Let's first begin by drawing on your spiritual strength given to you by your gracious heavenly Father. It's great news to realize that God never intended for you to live in pain from degenerative disease. The remaining portion of the book contains a powerful, anointed design for your pathway to healing—a plan to reverse the debilitating degenerative process.

As you look at the following protocols, prepare yourself mentally and emotionally to defeat whatever devastating condition is keeping you from being completely healthy. (See the other sections in the book for help in preparing mentally and emotionally.) I also want to assist you spiritually by including faith-building scriptural promises. I suggest you begin by praying this prayer:

> *Gracious Father, You are my God and my Protector. I seek You now and ask for courage and discipline to consistently apply the knowledge and information in this book to reverse this condition and restore my health. I am praising You and thanking You in advance for all Your natural and supernatural resources for my healing pathway. I praise Your holy name and thank You for giving me the courage and the fortitude to move forward even when I experience pain. Thank You for Your divine plan, Your healing Word and the life You gave me with a special purpose. Amen.*

I pray this prayer with and for you, and I will continue to covenant with you as you pursue the natural and spiritual resources I am providing for you here. My prayer is that this powerful plan will lead you along your healing pathway so that you can confidently and faithfully move away from the pain and discomfort of degenerative disease.

> **It's a great feeling to be grounded in your purpose for existence.**

Through this challenge, may you become stronger and more dedicated to identifying God's purpose for your life.

As you become stronger in spirit and faith, you will become more centered in understanding your purpose here on earth and more effective in serving God through serving others. The apostle Paul encouraged us:

> Since we find ourselves fashioned into all these excellently formed and marvelously functioning parts in Christ's body, let's just go ahead and be what we were made to be.
> —*Romans 12:5, THE MESSAGE*

It's a great feeling to be grounded in your purpose for existence; it just feels good to do what God put you here to do. So now, let's take a closer look at some specifics of where to go and what to do to be victorious over chronic, systemic conditions.

OSTEOPOROSIS

A loss of bone density would best describe this degenerative disease. There are a myriad of factors related to the onset and development of osteoporosis—factors such as genetics, surrounding environmental conditions and lifestyle, especially related to diet, exercise and digestive function.

Like most degenerative diseases and systemic conditions, the complication of osteoporosis begins many years before it is diagnosed. Osteoporosis is basically a metabolic bone disorder that slows the rate of bone formation and accelerates the rate of bone resorption, resulting in loss of bone mass. The loss of essential calcium and phosphate salts results in weak porous bone that is vulnerable to fractures in its brittle state. Osteoporosis is most common in women, due to long-term calcium loss during pregnancies and menstruation. Postmenopausal women are at greatest risk for this debilitating condition.

When calcium is present with little or no silica present, fractures do not knit. On the other hand, bones knit extremely well when there is little calcium but an abundance of silica. It was concluded that silica is the most important supplement in bone health, with manganese and potassium the next two in importance.

Osteoporosis can be very crippling in nature. The bones weaken as they lose their mineral content and become porous, causing one to become extremely vulnerable to fractures and injury. The good news is that God never intended for you to live in pain from the degeneration of your bones. He is good, and He responds to your every need and wants you to be whole and pain free. God promised to respond when we call on Him:

> Call to me and I will answer you and tell you great and unsearchable things you do not know.
>
> —*Jeremiah 33:3, NIV*

Special considerations for osteoporosis

The following suggestions may apply to more conditions than osteoporosis, but they are especially helpful for this condition. I recommend that you take time to make a list of specific ways you will apply these suggestions to your lifestyle. Keeping a record will encourage you to be consistent and will help you to mark your progress.

The natural approach. Exercise is a critical step to the prevention and/or the reversal process of osteoporosis. Exercise helps control bone loss by improving calcium absorption and stimulating bone formation.

The best exercises for strengthening and thickening the bones are weight-bearing exercises such as lifting weights or stretching bands for resistance, walking, cycling and calisthenics. The tendon head pull on the bone (where the muscle attaches to the bone) causes the bone to thicken and strengthen. Exercises such as push-ups, dips, squats, lunges and stretches will stress the bone and stimulate growth and regeneration of cells. Aerobic exercises, also including walking briskly or bouncing on a mini-trampoline, are excellent. (See the product page for ordering information for The Body Advantage Exercise System, and refer to the description of exercises in chapter eight.) You can also buy a set of dumbbells (5 to 10 pounds) for overhead presses, bicep curls or squats.

Osteoporosis primarily affects the hips, spine, arms and shoulders.

Osteoporosis primarily affects the hips, spine, arms and shoulders. Exercises designed to strengthen these bones, such as the ones suggested above, are extremely important. There are forms and charts in Part IV to record your exercise sessions and to keep you motivated.

If you are vulnerable to this disease, also consider how you can improve your nutritional regimen. And consider short, one-day fasts to help improve assimilation of nutrients. Blood purification and liver cleansing will help improve digestion. (See chapter five, "Step 2: Detoxify Your Body.") An excellent herb for cleansing the blood and liver is red clover.

Foods to consider for healing. Green leafy vegetables, salads and steamed veggies are good choices, along with brown rice, other whole grains and buckwheat, which are good sources of silica and magnesium. Other foods that are high in magnesium and calcium are almonds, sesame seeds, red beans, white beans, lima beans, soybeans, parsley, leafy greens and kelp. Fat-free milk is one of the best sources of calcium.

Vitamins, minerals and herbs. Phosphorous and vitamins A, C and D are helpful in the absorption of calcium. Fluorine is helpful in preventing bone loss and is found naturally in herbs. The ratio of calcium to phosphorous is important; therefore, care should be taken not to overload on phosphorous in your diet with sodas, refined foods and red meats.

There are a number of herbs that are helpful in balancing, absorbing and assimilating minerals as well as boosting the immune system so that these processes are more efficient. They include echinacea, garlic, red clover, black clover, alfalfa, horsetail, hawthorn and sarsaparilla, as well as goldenseal and ginseng.

Caution: Carbonation and sugar leech calcium from bones, so consumption should be limited.

The miracle nutrients. Lecithin, evening primrose oil and coenzyme Q_{10} improve circulation and prevent fatty deposits. Apple cider vinegar and oil of oregano are extremely effective for clearing and cleansing. Add 1 tablespoon of apple cider vinegar to your favorite juice each morning. An adequate dosage for oil of oregano is 10 to 20 drops under your tongue, adjusted as needed.

One of the wisest decisions you can make is to decide to follow a nutritional regimen that will help protect you from osteoporosis. Foods laden with calcium and magnesium are some of the healthiest we can choose from God's natural resources. As we have discussed, our diet should consist of 50 percent fresh fruits and veggies.

Be sure to modify carbonated drinks and red meat because they contain large amounts of phosphorous that leech calcium from the bones. Another important point is that without adequate amounts of magnesium (200–400 milligrams daily), the body will only absorb about 25 percent of the calcium available.

Spiritual assistance

Go to God's Word regularly to increase your faith for healing. God has promised to be there for you in times of need, especially when you are faced with trials and tribulation. If you are struggling with osteoporosis, you need strength, energy and discipline to overcome and return to health and vitality. As stated earlier, the following promises are among many that can strengthen you:

> You whom I have taken from the ends of the earth, and called from its farthest regions, and said to you, you are My servant, I have chosen you and have not cast you away: fear not, for I am with you; be not dismayed, for I am your God. I will strengthen you, yes, I will help you, I will uphold you with My righteous right hand.
>
> —*Isaiah 41:9–10*

> But those who wait on the LORD shall renew their strength; they shall mount up with wings like eagles, they shall run and not be weary, they shall walk and not faint.
>
> —*Isaiah 40:31*

A prayer for your healing pathway from God

> *Precious heavenly Father, You have already given me*
> *the power and the discipline to use the protocol in this*
> *book to overcome osteoporosis—please strengthen*
> *me and help me use it. (See 2 Timothy 1:7.) I praise*
> *You and thank You for creating me for a purpose.*
> *I pray that through my healing pathway I will more*
> *clearly discover and confirm my purpose here on*
> *earth. I will look forward to serving You through a*
> *healthier and stronger mind, body and spirit. Amen.*

ALZHEIMER'S DISEASE

Alzheimer's is a very debilitating and damaging degenerative disease. The onset of the condition is usually in the later senior years, typically in the late sixties, early seventies or even into the eighties and nineties. It is strongly suspected that Alzheimer's disease is another degenerative condition that may have an immune connection. This disease slowly and progressively

> **I am firmly convinced that Alzheimer's is brought on by abusive lifestyles and toxic environment.**

attacks the nerve cells of the brain and gradually results in the loss of memory and cognitive thinking. Research scientists are currently researching the role that the immune system plays in causing the disease when it produces an overabundance of the amino acid glutamate, a powerful nerve-cell killer.

Another theory under investigation is the suspicion that Alzheimer's disease could possibly be triggered in part by a virus. This idea came from the discovery that those who are already genetically predisposed to Alzheimer's and have a compromised immune system are more vulnerable to a virus such as herpes, which could lead to the onset of Alzheimer's.

Contrary to the above theories, I am firmly convinced that Alzheimer's is brought on by abusive lifestyles and toxic environment—the very same factors that cause strokes, diabetes, high blood pressure, high cholesterol, heart disease and cancer.

But remember, God does not want for you to live with the challenge that Alzheimer's disease presents. His desire is for you to be healthy and strong. He is good, and He responds to your every need and wants you to be whole and pain free. Before you pursue the protocol listed below, ask Him for strength. Jesus declared:

> Come to me, all you who labor and are heavy laden, and I
> will give you rest.
>
> —*Matthew 11:28*

Consider this protocol now as a preventive measure to fight against the potential for Alzheimer's disease you could possibly face in the future.

Special considerations for Alzheimer's disease

As you prayerfully consider how to prevent this disease or restore health to your mind, please include the following suggestions for your treatment protocol.

The natural approach. Exercising regularly is extremely important for those in the senior years to help ward off Alzheimer's disease along with other degenerative conditions. As we have discussed, the best exercises for those in their senior years are stretching, weight-bearing and resistance exercises with either weights or stretch bands for resistance and finally, aerobic-type exercises such as walking, swimming, cycling and calisthenics. The blood flow and oxygenation process increased by exercise stimulates cell cleansing and regeneration in the brain, imperative for fighting Alzheimer's. (Please refer to the product page for The Body Advantage Exercise System, and see the description of exercises in chapter eight.)

Get moving on a daily basis; exercise enhances blood flow, bringing to the brain the oxygen and nutrients it needs to function well. This increased blood flow cleans out toxins, LDL cholesterol and other metabolic waste that would form plaque and create blockage to cause memory problems, dementia and other pre-Alzheimer's symptoms. In my opinion, one

People with high levels of activity are three and one-half times less likely to get Alzheimer's.

of the most important things we can do as we age is to simply walk. My recommendation still stands. As I have said, walk your dog every day, whether you have one or not.

A landmark study conducted by Dr. David Snowden, a professor of Neurology at the University of Kentucky Medical Center for the past sixteen years, further validates the positive benefits of exercise.[1]

This study is among the most important of its kind in helping to unlock the long-held secrets of Alzheimer's disease. One of the significant findings of the study is that what's good for the heart also tends to be good for the brain, so by controlling things such as blood pressure, cholesterol levels and body weight, people also are helping to control their risk for Alzheimer's disease. Another significant finding was that exercise reduces stress hormones and increases chemicals that nourish brain cells, which can help ward off depression and some kinds of damage to brain tissue.

Exercise also helps to prevent strokes, diabetes, high blood pressure, high cholesterol, heart disease and cancer, all of which can elevate Alzheimer's disease risk. In a study reported in the Proceedings of the National Academy of Sciences, it was found that people with high levels of activity were about three and one-half times less likely to get Alzheimer's disease than those with lower levels of activity.[2]

Foods to consider for healing. Use distilled water, which has a chelating effect on the arteries and veins. Other foods that have a chelating effect are cabbage, turnip, spinach, onions, garlic, kelp, raspberry, brussels sprouts and watercress. Keeping a lot of fiber in the diet is also very important, along with beta carotene and the cruciferous vegetables. Green salads, fresh veggies (such as carrots and asparagus), fresh fruits (especially citrus fruits), seeds, nuts and cold-pressed oils (such as virgin olive oil and grapeseed oil) are also very beneficial.

Scientists measure a food's antioxidant potential in units called "oxygen radical absorbency capacities" (ORACs). While the USDA estimates that most of us currently take in only about 1,200 ORACs daily, the Tufts University researchers recommend at least 3,500 ORACs daily and preferably between 5,000–6,000, just to play it safe. Tufts University researchers have identified a list of fruits and vegetables with the highest ORACs that are our best antioxidant sources. The following is a list of fruits and vegetables that should be eaten on a regular basis and are great sources of not only disease-fighting antioxidants, but also very important vitamins, minerals and fiber. These powerful antioxidant fruits and vegetables will buffer free radicals and help to ward off Alzheimer's disease as well as other systemic conditions: blueberries, blackberries, strawberries, spinach, kale, raisins, oranges, cranberries, broccoli florets, plums, grapefruit, red bell pepper, raspberries, beets, cantaloupe and beans of many varieties.

While the fruits and veggies just listed are our very best antioxidant sources, the following foods should also be included in the diet whenever possible for protection: apples, cherries, prunes, grapes, peas, kidney beans, cauliflower, apricots, brussels sprouts, kiwi fruit, onions, garlic, carrots, yellow squash, zucchini, tomatoes, leaf lettuce, peaches, bananas and corn.

Vitamins, minerals and herbs. Because vitamin E assists in transporting oxygen to the brain cells, it is one of the nutrients that may prevent the onset of Alzheimer's. Aluminum is one of the suspected culprits in Alzheimer's. Levels of aluminum in the body may be reduced by vitamin C, the B-complex vitamins (especially thiamine), calcium and magnesium.

It is known that minerals are essential for a healthy nervous system and brain. Some of those that play a vital role are zinc, iodine, magnesium, manganese, selenium and copper. Sulfur and phosphorus are also needed to nourish the brain and nervous system.

Herbs such as ginger, ginseng and ginkgo can improve concentration and enhance memory and brain function. Lady's slipper feeds the nervous system, while prickly ash and passionflower increase circulation and help to clean arteries. Use psyllium to clean the colon of toxins that eventually work their way to the brain if not cleansed.

Also, taking lecithin stimulates the production of acetylcholine, which improves short-term memory. My Twenty-one-Day Detoxification Program, along with oral chelation using herbs, vitamins and minerals, will help to clear the arteries and veins.

The miracle nutrients. Coenzyme Q_{10} transports oxygen to the brain more efficiently. Bee pollen and lecithin, along with salmon oil and free-form amino acids, also enhance brain function. Spirulina, chlorella and blue-green algae absorb the heavy metals and help protect against aluminum, mercury and lead.

> There is a definite link between low levels of folic acid in the blood and increased risk of brain atrophy.

Apple cider vinegar and oil of oregano are extremely effective for clearing and cleansing. Add 1 tablespoon of apple cider vinegar to your favorite juice each morning. An adequate dosage of oil of oregano is 10 to 20 drops under your tongue, adjusted as needed.

Folic acid and lycopene are two other miracle nutrients that have begun attracting attention for their ability to help prevent Alzheimer's disease. As far back as the 1970s it was observed that mothers giving birth to babies with birth defects had low levels of folic acid. Most recently, this finding was also identified in Dr. Snowden's study, where he found a definite link between low levels of folic acid in the blood and increased risk of brain atrophy, which is typical of Alzheimer's disease. Dr. Snowden also found in women between the ages of seventy-seven and ninety-eight that those with the highest levels of lycopene in their blood were four times less likely to need assistance with such activities as walking, dressing, bathing and feeding themselves than those whose lycopene levels were the lowest.[3]

Lycopene, a powerful antioxidant, is plentiful in tomatoes. Therefore, some of the products to be consumed for protection against Alzheimer's would be tomato ketchup, spaghetti sauce, tomato sauce, tomato soup, tomato juice, vegetable juice and canned tomatoes, as well as fresh tomatoes.

Green tea and black tea should also be consumed since they are right up there with such antioxidant powerhouses as strawberries and spinach. Black tea has a few more antioxidants in it than green tea; however, green tea contains an extremely powerful antioxidant called *epigallocatechin gallate* (EGCG), which makes green tea probably the better choice for reducing Alzheimer's disease risk.

Spiritual assistance

God will provide you with the strength you need by drawing on His promises. Go to His Word to find those promises. The Bible declares that His Word is a lamp for your feet and a light for your path. (See Psalm 119:105.) He will be there for you in times of need. The psalmist experienced this reality:

> I waited patiently for the LORD to help me, and he turned to me and heard my cry. He lifted me out of the pit of despair, out of the mud and the mire. He set my feet on solid ground and steadied me as I walked along. He has given me a new song to sing, a hymn of praise to our God. Many will see what he has done and be astounded. They will put their trust in the LORD.
>
> *—Psalm 40:1–3, NLT*

> Give all your worries and cares to God, for he cares about what happens to you.
>
> *—1 Peter 5:7, NLT*

A prayer for your healing pathway from God

Precious heavenly Father, thank You for the power and

*the discipline You have already given me to use the
protocol in this book to fight Alzheimer's disease—
strengthen me and help me use it. (See 2 Timothy 1:7.)
I know that by pursuing a healthy lifestyle, I will be
more aware of the purpose for which You created me.
As I become healthier and stronger, I know that I will
covet that purpose. I praise You now for the healing
You will bring about in my life and will give You the
glory as I am able to better serve You through a
healthier mind, body and spirit. Amen.*

CHRONIC FATIGUE AND FIBROMYALGIA

A tragic reality within our societal structure has been that when most
people complain of early morning stiffness, muscle pain, weakness and
lack of an ability to sleep soundly, doctors and sometimes family
and friends dismiss the problem as imaginary. Fortunately, chronic
fatigue syndrome (CFS) and fibromyalgia are beginning to be recognized as actual illnesses.

Most people who have CFS also manifest most of the symptoms of fibromyalgia, which affects millions of people of all ages
in America. In my personal experience, I have worked with people
demonstrating these symptoms ranging from the ages of nine to
ninety.

As I discuss in my book *Reversing Fibromyalgia,*[4] fibromyalgia
is a medical condition that affects the fibrous connective tissue surrounding the muscle. It is said to be a form of muscular and "soft
tissue" rheumatism, rather than arthritis of the joints. Fibromyalgia
mainly affects muscles and their attachments to bones, especially in
areas of muscle/tendon junctions. A more complete list of symptoms
is as follows:

- Generalized aches and/or stiffness of at least three
  to six anatomical sites, persisting for at least three
  months

- Six or more typical reproducible soft tissue tender
  points

- Generalized chronic fatigue

- Chronic headaches

- Sleep disturbance—inability to reach deep sleep

- Neurological difficulties (frequent eye prescription changes, blurred vision, difficulty calculating numbers, etc.)

- Soft tissue and joint swelling

- Numbing and tingling sensations in the fingers and the toes (disautonomia)

- Irritable bowel syndrome

- Varied symptoms in relation to weather changes, stress, trauma and physical activity

Special considerations for chronic fatigue syndrome and fibromyalgia

Thankfully, God does not intend for you to live with the pain and exhaustion you now experience as a result of chronic fatigue syndrome or fibromyalgia. As one former sufferer exuberantly proclaims, "I read your protocol in one night, and my life hasn't been the same since...As I began putting these steps into my lifestyle, the results were amazing...You honestly saved my life." Carefully consider the following suggestions for rebuilding your health.

The natural approach. With a sound nutrition program and proper cleansing, the body will gain strength and energy. It sometimes requires months and years for the healing process. Patience, persistence and positive thinking will expedite the process. Chronic fatigue and fibromyalgia carry symptoms of a toxic body with toxic cells that cannot assimilate nutrients for energy. Therefore, it is imperative that the healing process starts with cleansing of the cells and body. My Twenty-one-Day Detoxification Program, along with blood purifiers and colon cleansers, will give you a jump-start toward the healing process.

Begin exercising once you start gaining strength. It is extremely important to realize that exercise is definitely one of the most powerful medicines available. The most valuable investment you can make to your good health and to the healing process is the time that you spend exercising. (Please see Part IV for exercise protocols, forms and charts.) I have provided for you all of the information you need to help you develop and personalize your own exercise program.

As part of the natural approach to healing these conditions, follow my guidelines for returning to deep sleep and getting back in balance. Chiropractic treatments to balance the nervous system can also be extremely helpful.

Foods to consider for healing. Fresh steamed and raw fruits and veggies are an excellent place to start as they contain minerals for synthesizing energy, cleansing, balancing and healing. Whole grains, seeds (such as pumpkinseeds, flaxseeds and sunflower seeds) and nuts (such as cashews, almonds and pecans) help the balancing and healing process.

Vitamins, minerals and herbs. It has been discovered that magnesium and malic acid from apples are an amazing synergistic formula for nourishing the muscle and internal body tissues to eliminate nagging pain and the flu-like feeling that accompanies chronic fatigue and fibromyalgia. This combination also refuels the energy cycle (Kreb's cycle) and assists in balancing for getting back to deep sleep (level 4) where the body can complete the job of healing.

Vitamins A, C and E (the vitamin antioxidants) are extremely important along with the B complexes. The amino acid chains are also important, serving as precursors to major hormones for balance. The compound 5-hydroxytryptophan (5-HTP) also works well to stimulate serotonin, which produces melatonin from the pineal gland for relaxation and sleep. Lipoic acid, biotin and inositol are also helpful supplements for these conditions.

The miracle nutrients. Grape seed extract, rice bran extract, coenzyme Q_{10} and green and black tea are excellent nutrients that promote healing, as well as goldenseal, organic apple cider vinegar and oil of oregano for cleansing and a natural antibiotic effect. Add 1 tablespoon of apple cider vinegar to your favorite juice each morning. Oil of oregano is also healing; an adequate dosage of oil of oregano is 10 to 20 drops under your tongue, adjusted as needed.

Magnesium is a critically important nutrient for fibromyalgia and chronic fatigue syndrome because in nearly 100 percent of the cases, low magnesium levels are traditionally found with these conditions. Magnesium is critical to many cellular functions, protein formation and cellular replication, as well as energy production. It participates in more than 300 enzymatic reactions in the body, particularly those processes that produce energy in the Krebs cycle where adenosine triphosphate (ATP) is produced. The key factor here is that whenever magnesium levels are low, energy levels are low—magnesium being the primary energy component for the human energy cycle. Magnesium and malic acid supplementation have produced excellent results in treating fibromyalgia and chronic fatigue syndrome. The positive effect in these patients is more than likely due to magnesium's critical importance in the secretion of serotonin. Serotonin is a brain neuropeptide, which is the major precursor for producing melatonin for relaxation and sleep, as we mentioned.

Along with recommending supplementation of magnesium as a nutrient, I also encourage increasing the intake of magnesium in the diet. One of the wisest decisions you can make is to decide to follow a nutritional regimen that will help protect you from fibromyalgia/CFS. Foods laden with calcium and magnesium are some of the healthiest we can choose from God's natural resources. Let me mention again that our diet should consist of 50 percent fresh fruits and veggies. Along with the suggestions I have made above, follow the general guidelines listed at the beginning of the chapter for a healthy diet.

Some of the better food sources for magnesium are green leafy vegetables, whole grains, fish, skim milk, seeds, nuts, tofu, beans, lentils and legumes. One of the major reasons for low magnesium levels in most Americans is that the nutritional diet here is made of such highly refined foods, fast foods, meat and high-fat dairy products.

Although magnesium can be most effective on its own, I recommend that it be taken synergistically with other nutrients such as calcium and vitamins C and D, so that it will be absorbed effectively and efficiently. This works much more efficiently because when nutrients are combined in a synergistic formula, they become much more powerful than if taken alone. For a therapeutic effect, I recommend a very potent multivitamin with amino acid chains that can act as precursors to the major hormones, as well as the human growth hormone. Also, magnesium mixed with malic acid is extremely powerful as a cleanser, as a body tissue nourisher and as a refurbisher of the energy cycle.

The dosage recommended for magnesium on a daily basis is 400 milligrams when building up from a deficiency, and then once a buildup has been achieved, the dosage may be reduced. I also recommend 400 to 800 milligrams of malic acid along with the magnesium on a daily basis. A human growth hormone product is also recommended, along with an excellent product to buffer the body's pH.

Spiritual assistance

Take courage from the promises God gives you, such as: "Casting all your care upon Him, for He cares for you" (1 Pet. 5:7). Examine the following protocol and take the challenge to defeat these potentially devastating conditions. Look to His Word for faith-building promises, and review the prayers and scriptures included in this book as you begin your path to healing. This protocol, along with the strength you draw from God, will reverse the effects of these diseases. You can declare confidently with the psalmist:

> You are holding my right hand. You will keep on guiding me with your counsel, leading me to a glorious destiny.
> —*Psalm 73:23–24*, NLT

As God holds your hand, I continue to pray for you. As He keeps on guiding you with His counsel, I encourage you to apply the information here that you need to become strong and healthy again. You will again be able to serve others, and as you lift Christ up through this service, you will draw others to Him. Then you will clearly understand the purpose for which he created you. The Scriptures explain this reality clearly:

> God has given gifts to each of you from his great variety of spiritual gifts. Manage them well so that God's generosity can flow through you…Do [them] with all the strength and energy that God supplies. Then God will be given glory in everything through Jesus Christ.
> —*1 Peter 4:10–11*, NLT

As you begin this path to healing by following the suggestions in this protocol, begin also to thank the Lord for the victory He will give you as you defeat CFS or fibromyalgia. God's Word will provide you with the wisdom and the strength you will need to follow this plan. For example, He promises:

> Do not be afraid, for I have ransomed you. I have called you by name; you are mine. When you go through deep waters and great trouble, I will be with you. When you go through rivers of difficulty, you will not drown! When you walk through the fire of oppression, you will not be burned up…For I am the LORD, your God, the Holy One of Israel, your Savior.
> —*Isaiah 43:1–3*, NLT

But the LORD still waits for you to come to him so he can show you his love and compassion. For the LORD is a faithful God. Blessed are those who wait for him to help them.

—*Isaiah 30:18, NLT*

A prayer for your healing pathway from God

> *Father God, thank You for the power and discipline that You have already given me to use the protocol given to me in this book to overcome fibromyalgia/ chronic fatigue syndrome. (See 2 Timothy 1:7.) Give me the strength according to Your promises, and help me use this anointed plan to restore my health. I praise You that as I wait on You I will find new strength. Through this new strength, help me discover the purpose for which You created me, the purpose only I have according to Your divine plan. For You created my inmost being; I praise You because I am fearfully and wonderfully made. As I heal, I will look forward to serving You and others through a healthier and stronger mind, body and spirit. Amen.*

CROHN'S DISEASE

Crohn's disease is by far the most serious of the digestive tract ills and is extremely difficult to treat. Crohn's is suspected to be caused by an autoimmune reaction and is most likely from a virus or a particular strain of bacteria. Since Crohn's tends to run in families, it reflects a genetic connection as well.[5]

Those who suffer with Crohn's disease experience an ongoing inflammation of the lining of the intestine. Inflammation affects the walls of the intestine, gradually scarring them, causing them to thicken and become prone to blockage. Symptoms of Crohn's are very similar to other intestinal conditions such as ulcerative colitis and irritable bowel syndrome.

Symptoms for Crohn's disease include:

- Dry skin
- Fatigue
- Muscle weakness
- Painful abdominal bloating

- Hair loss
- Anemia
- Diarrhea
- Weight loss

The exciting news is that God does not intend for you to suffer as a result of Crohn's disease. His desire for you is that you are healthy so that you may better serve Him and others. In the following section, you will discover a natural way to overcome this debilitating disease, but before you begin, take a moment to review the prayer and scripture at the beginning of this chapter. You will need to be prepared mentally, emotionally and, above all, spiritually as you begin your healing pathway. Know also that I am praying for you so that you can overcome Crohn's. And as you become well, you will more clearly discover the purpose God has for you. God desires to bless you, as His Word declares:

> Blessed is the man who walks not in the counsel of the ungodly, nor stands in the path of sinners, nor sits in the seat of the scornful; but his delight is in the law of the LORD, and in His law he meditates day and night. He shall be like a tree planted by the rivers of water, that brings forth its fruit in its season.
>
> *Psalm 1:1–3*

Special considerations for Crohn's disease

As you make the determined decision to restore and maintain health, the following protocol will help you to achieve your goals.

The natural approach. Overwhelm the system with fluids such as distilled water, wheat and barley grass juice, freshly squeezed juices and cleansing herbal teas. The goal for good nutrition here is to cleanse the body of toxins, work to improve digestion, flush out parasites, replace good bacteria and microflora and build the immune system.

Foods to consider for healing. Make soft, healing foods such as oatmeal and mush. Consume vegetable and meat broths for vitamins, minerals and protein that are needed. Try steamed vegetables, including cruciferous veggies like brussels sprouts, cauliflower, broccoli, kale and cabbage, and throw in carrots as well. Since Crohn's is suspected to be related to a lack of beneficial bacteria, try yogurt with live cultures. Finally, since it's considered an acidic condition, take foods that are low in acid and are more alkaline to balance the pH (potential hydrogen quotient). Take a look at the pH balancing suggestions at the beginning of this chapter, and see the product page for ordering information for an excellent pH-balancing product.

Vitamins, minerals and herbs. There is a need to replace B-complex vitamins. Poor absorption of foods and nutrients is the major problem with this disease, and B-vitamin deficiencies are most common. Also replenish with vitamins A, C and E to boost the immune system and to fight infection. A good multivitamin is essential.

The miracle nutrients. I must list aloe vera as one of the truly miracle nutrients. Evening primrose oil, flaxseed oil and the chlorophyll foods such as spirulina, chlorella and blue-green algae are also extremely helpful to heal the intestines.

It is my opinion that after years of poor eating habits, lack of exercise, a long string of medications and poor health habits in general, the gastrointestinal tract becomes so unhealthy that the immune system becomes very compromised and confused. One theory for the cause of Crohn's disease is that the immune system then begins to attack the toxic tissues with the objective to destroy them, thinking they are a foreign organism, when in fact they are simply their own toxic tissues. The conclusion, then, is that parasites and autointoxication are two of the main causes of Crohn's disease.

For that reason a nutritional therapy for Crohn's disease deserves special attention. A diet free of meat historically has helped tremendously with Crohn's patients, as meat can cause parasite infestation and chronic constipation. A high-fiber diet is most beneficial, while simultaneously eliminating white flour and white sugar products. A good, solid program of consuming foods that are building, cleaning and healing will provide nutrients that have been lacking.

Some additional herbs that help the healing process significantly with this dilemma are black walnut, goldenseal, kelp, passion flower, fenugreek, bee pollen, alfalfa, pau d'arco, cascara sagrada, burdock, white oak bark, slippery elm and psyllium. Acidophilus is essential for healing of the colon and for replacing the friendly bacteria that have been flushed out by the problems with Crohn's. Trace minerals in extract form are also extremely beneficial for healing in this case. Liquid chlorophyll is very healing and rich in vitamins and minerals for the healing process, especially vitamin K.

Spiritual assistance

God's promises in His Word will provide you with help as you begin this healing pathway. The Bible declares that your faith to receive God's promises will grow as you hear His message to you. (See Romans 10:17.) He has promised that He will not forsake you when you call to Him. (See Deuteronomy 4:31.) And you will need to call on Him now for strength and discipline as you begin your journey to healing. Consider these wonderful promises and begin to let your heart receive them:

> Those who know your name trust in you, for you, O LORD, have never abandoned anyone who searches for you.
>
> —*Psalm 9:10, NLT*

> The LORD is my rock, my fortress, and my savior; my God is my rock, in whom I find protection. He is my shield, the strength of my salvation, and my stronghold.
>
> —*Psalm 18:2, NLT*

A prayer for your healing pathway from God

> *Father God, thank You for already giving me the power and discipline to utilize the protocol in this book to overcome Crohn's disease. (See 2 Timothy 1:7.) Now I ask for the strength to help me use it. I praise You for the special purpose for which You created me. As I become whole again, I know that I will be able to better serve You and others, lifting up Your holy name so that others will be drawn to You. And I will glorify You for my renewed health. Amen.*

LUPUS

Systemic lupus erythematosus (SLE) is more commonly known as lupus, which is the Latin word for *wolf*. The name was derived from one of the disease's most common symptoms, a red facial rash that resembles a wolf's snout.

Lupus is an aggressive systemic condition that attacks other parts of the body besides the skin. The body appears to become allergic to itself, with the joints, central nervous system, kidneys, heart and lungs also placed at risk.

Lupus affects approximately one and one-half million people in the United States, with 90 percent of those diagnosed with the disease being women. Eighty percent of those afflicted with lupus develop the disease between the ages of fifteen and forty-five. Lupus is also two to three times more prevalent among African Americans, Hispanics, Asians and Native Americans.[6] Symptoms of lupus include:

- Tenderness in the joints
- Joint swelling
- Allergic-like skin eruptions
- Malaise
- Joint pains
- Fever
- Hair loss
- Fatigue
- Spontaneous bruising
- "Butterfly" rash on face
- Depression

A compromised immune system is recognized as one of the causes of lupus. Mental and/or physical stress, immunizations, viral infections and pregnancy may all also affect the development of lupus. One particular problem with stress is that it weakens the adrenal glands, producing a pseudo-hypoglycemic effect on the body. Lupus is recognized as an autoimmune disease, which is literally an abnormal reaction of the body to its own tissues.

Parasites also appear to be a problem with lupus; most often the droppings that parasites excrete in the body become toxic and prevent healing until they are eliminated. Until the blood stream is cleansed of parasites, healing cannot really take place.

Allergies can also be involved with lupus. The immune system becomes so weakened that the mucous membranes cannot tolerate everything that they come in contact with.

As debilitating as this disease is, find comfort in the fact that God does not want you to suffer from it. His honest desire is for you to be healthy. His Word promises that He will restore, support and strengthen you, and He will place you on a firm foundation. (See 1 Peter 5:10, NLT.) This section contains a powerful, anointed design for your healing, a pathway to reverse the debilitating effects of lupus.

Special considerations for lupus

Before you begin to assimilate this healing protocol, I encourage you to ask God for the power and strength to follow the plan. Consider again the prayer and scripture at the beginning of the chapter for reassurance. Also, prepare yourself mentally and emotionally to defeat this devastating condition. Prayerfully consider the scriptures I have included here that will boost your faith in yourself and God, who will give you the strength you need to overcome lupus.

The natural approach. Exercise is strongly recommended along with massage of the extremities. This therapy assists the body greatly in getting rid of toxins. A change of diet would be the next consideration. One of the ways (maybe the only way) to heal this disease is to consume large amounts of naturally cleansing foods such as raw fruits and veggies. Bowel and liver cleansers are in order, along with herbal blood purifiers that kill worms and parasites.

Foods to consider for healing. Almonds, sunflower seeds, pumpkinseeds, brown rice, barley, wheat grass, whole rolled oats, whole grains, lentils and beans are all extremely healthful foods to be consumed in generous portions.

A very critical factor here is to get the immune system strengthened, so a diet very high in vegetables, fruits, grains, green salads, sprouts and brown rice will help to strengthen the immune system and also cleanse the blood. Also eat green salads with lemon, olive oil and grape seed oil dressing. Include salmon, cabbage, broccoli, avocados and parsley in your diet. Vegetable juice fasting using chlorella, barley grass, wheat grass, and spirulina will also help to cleanse the blood, strengthen the immune system and balance the body's pH.

Vitamins, minerals and herbs. B-complex vitamins with PABA (para aminobenzoic acid) are very effective. Vitamins A and C with bioflavonoids are essential for boosting the immune system and strengthening connective tissues. Magnesium and calcium along with the trace minerals selenium, zinc and silicon are essential for getting well. Pau d'arco, burdock and red clover are good for cleansing the blood and liver. Goldenseal and black walnut will assist in killing worms and parasites. Echinacea, fenugreek and oat straw help to cleanse also.

The miracle nutrients. Salmon oil, evening primrose oil, grape seed oil and fish oils provide much needed omega-3 and omega-6 essential fatty acids. Coenzyme Q_{10} is an excellent addition for circulation and transporting oxygen. Oil of oregano will also aid with worms, parasites and bacteria as well as perform as a natural antibiotic. Dosage for oil of oregano should begin with 3 to 4 drops daily under the tongue, adding more as needed depending on the individual needs. Organic apple cider vinegar is helpful; 1 tablespoon a day in 4 ounces of apple juice is adequate.

The colon should be cleansed thoroughly, as this is where toxins accumulate; if not cleansed, the toxins will be redistributed into the blood stream, which can cause other diseases. A few of the herbs that will boost the immune system are ginkgo, ginseng, cayenne, suma and gotu kola. Other important substances are the omega-3 fatty acids, and some of the better sources are ground flaxseeds, flaxseed oil and salmon oil. These particular fatty acids are extremely effective for ridding the body of inflammation. Chlorophyll and blue-green algae are very helpful in the absorption of nutrients and boosting the immune system. These green substances also help to clean the blood and the liver of toxins. Finally, calcium and magnesium, which I discussed earlier, are necessary for the health of the nerves and the connective tissues.

Spiritual assistance

Faith and determination are major factors, as we have mentioned, in overcoming a degenerative disease like lupus. The outcome depends heavily on the emotional, physical and spiritual strength of the individual. Survival and healing will be determined largely by your faith and mental attitude. Scripture provides the strength and perspective you need to build your faith:

> For God has not given us a spirit of fear and timidity, but of power, love, and self-discipline.
>
> —2 *Timothy 1:7*, NLT

> Therefore I say to you, whatever things you ask when you pray, believe that you receive them, and you will have them.
>
> —*Mark 11:24*

You will find the strength you need in God's Word. Take comfort in knowing His promises will uplift and encourage you when you are in need. Changing your lifestyle to become healthy and whole again will require strength greater than what you alone possess, so now is a time of need when you can draw upon the strength that comes only from Him. Know that as you seek His counsel, He will bless you with the discipline to return to health and vitality and overcome lupus. And remember that I continue to pray for you, as well. I claim God's promise that He will renew your strength, agreeing with you that you will be restored as you follow this plan and trust in Him. Consider these wonderful promises:

Do not be afraid or discouraged, for the LORD is the one who goes before you. He will be with you; he will neither fail you nor forsake you.

—*Deuteronomy 31:8, NLT*

For since the world began, no ear has heard, and no eye has seen a God like you, who works for those who wait for him!

—*Isaiah 64:4, NLT*

A prayer for your healing pathway from God

Father God, I praise You, for You have already given me the power and the discipline to use the protocol given to me in this book to overcome lupus— strengthen me and help me use it. (See 2 Timothy 1:7.) Thank You that this promise and all of Your promises are true and that You are a shield for all who look to You for protection. (See 2 Samuel 22:31.) I know I am not here by accident; You created me to commune with You. As I heal, I thank You for the opportunity I have to commune with You more, waiting on You in prayer and thanksgiving. As I recover my health and determine to serve You and others, I will give You the glory for my renewed strength, so that others may be drawn to You through me. Amen.

RAYNAUD'S DISEASE

Raynaud's disease is characterized by a change in the color of the skin to white, then blue and finally red as warmth returns. It is considered to have an autoimmune connection manifested by painfully cold fingers and toes. The onset is most often triggered by a rapid change in temperature, particularly cold. At times this trigger can be as simple as touching a frosted window on a cold morning. The blood flow to the small capillaries of the fingers and toes is cut off as a result. Other symptoms include:

One of the gifts God is so eager to give you is the restoration of your health.

- Brittle nails (caused from impaired circulation)
- Cold hands and/or feet

- Numbness
- Tingling
- Fingers first turn white, then blue, and finally red

Draw comfort in knowing that God does not want for you to suffer with the symptoms of Raynaud's. His plan for your life is one of health and vitality. One of the gifts God is so eager to give you is the restoration of your health. (See Jeremiah 30:17.) We know that we need to ask Him to help us on our healing pathway, but we also need to commit to a plan of action that has been proven successful.

Special considerations for Raynaud's disease

The protocol you are about to read is an effective plan of action. Together with your determination and the strength you draw from God, you will be able to reverse the effects of Raynaud's. Prepare yourself mentally and emotionally, taking a minute to reflect on the prayer and scripture at the beginning of this chapter. Know that I am praying for you—that you will be successful, whole and well, and therefore able to better serve God and others.

The natural approach. Exercising to enhance circulation, as well as cleansing and boosting the immune system, is essential to the natural treatment of Raynaud's disease. Add as many organic and natural foods as possible, including raw fruits and veggies. Be sure to reduce or eliminate entirely fatty fried foods. (See my Twenty-one-Day Detoxification Program on page 67.)

Foods to consider for healing. Add large quantities of fresh and raw fruits and veggies along with whole grains and increased fiber in the diet. Whole grains, nuts and seeds work together to ward off disease. Flaxseeds, pumpkinseeds, sunflower seeds, almonds and cashews are excellent choices. One of the effective methods of helping rid the body of toxins in the arteries is a high-fiber diet, especially one that includes psyllium. Some of the better fiber foods are fruits, vegetables, sprouts, whole grains, lentils, beans, nuts, seeds and herbs. Slow cooking of grains is important since this helps to retain the enzymes for proper digestion.

Vitamins, minerals and herbs. Vitamins A, C and E are needed to boost the immune system and improve circulation. L-arginine and niacin will assist in circulation by dilating the small blood vessels. Also try garlic, ginkgo, passionflower and butcher's broom to improve circulation and strengthen the arteries.

As with other degenerative diseases, apple cider vinegar and oil of oregano are extremely effective for clearing and cleansing. I recommend that you add 1 tablespoon of apple cider vinegar to your favorite juice each morning. An adequate dosage for oil of oregano is 10 to 20 drops under your tongue, adjusted as needed.

Some of the other herbs effective in improving blood flow are butchers broom, suma and gingko. Gotu kola, ginger, ephedra, ginseng, horsetail and hawthorn are all also very beneficial.

Be sure to incorporate into your plan the general nutrition information at the beginning of this chapter. Maintaining a balanced and healthy diet low in chemicals and processed food is important for improving any degenerative condition.

Spiritual assistance

It is important that you refer to God's Word for inspiration and help in becoming disciplined in following any regimen. He will give you direction and understanding, as promised in the Scriptures. (See Psalm 119:130.) His Word will always be there for you, giving you strength as you change your lifestyle to overcome Raynaud's. Claim His promises for yourself and your situation, and rejoice in knowing He hears you and delights in your commitment to Him and to a healthy lifestyle. Consider these wonderful promises:

> And now I entrust you to God and the word of his grace—
> his message that is able to build you up and give you an
> inheritance with all those he has set apart for himself.
>
> —*Acts 20:32,* NLT

> Without wavering, let us hold tightly to the hope we say
> we have, for God can be trusted to keep his promise.
>
> —*Hebrews 10:23,* NLT

A prayer for your healing pathway from God

> *Father God, I praise Your holy name for the power
> and discipline I already possess as a gift from You to
> overcome Raynaud's disease. (See 2 Timothy 1:7.)
> Please now give me the strength that comes only
> from You so that I may be disciplined to use this protocol.
> As I heal, help me to be more aware of the purpose
> You have laid out for me here on earth. I thank
> You for the ability I will have to better serve You and
> others as You heal my body, mind and spirit. Amen.*

SKIN DISEASES
(SCLERODERMA AND PSORIASIS)

The skin is the largest organ of the body and serves the vital function, among others, of eliminating pollution, gases, toxins and vapor from the body. About one-half gallon of toxins is eliminated daily by the skin if the pores are clean and free from dead cells. These toxins are forced back into the body if the pores are closed as a result of dead cell buildup. The body is then placed in an "overload" mode as the other elimination systems try to take over and help.

Skin diseases are toxic irritations manifested through the skin. If the body is overwhelmed with toxins, inflammation and fat deposits, the other cleansing organs—the liver, kidneys and digestive tract— cannot process and eliminate quickly enough. This causes the body to revert back to eliminating toxic wastes through the skin. Once again, when the skin is not properly cleansed, the perspiration, bacteria, rancid oils, dead skin and other waste materials accumulate and may result in blackheads, whiteheads, pimples and other skin diseases.

Scleroderma

This autoimmune disorder is characterized by hardening (*sclero*) of the skin (*derma*), usually on the fingers, hands, forearm and face. It is believed that this condition is a subtle form of arthritis. The cause of scleroderma is not clearly understood, though many interesting possibilities are under investigation as of this writing. An overproduction of collagen as a result of an autoimmune response is one very interesting characteristic of this condition.

In people without scleroderma, the immune system normally sparks cells to make collagen and create a scar as part of healing after an injury or infection. In people with scleroderma, the immune system sends mistaken signals, instructing connective tissue cells to produce collagen when it's not needed. Scar tissue then builds up unnecessarily, causing tightness and pain in the skin.

Psoriasis

One of the basic causes of psoriasis lies within the skin cells themselves. The rate at which cells divide is controlled by a delicate balance between two internally controlled compounds—cyclic AMP and cyclic GMP. Both decreased AMP and increased GMP have been measured in the skin of individuals with psoriasis. The result is excessive cell proliferation, causing new skin cells to develop too rapidly and pushing the cells above them outward. Normally it takes twenty-eight days to complete this cycle. However, for patients with psoriasis the cycle is completed in four days. The cells are being produced so rapidly they begin to stack up on the surface of the skin, causing thick, red patches covered with silvery scales. These patches usually appear on the scalp, face, knees, elbows, lower back, buttocks, palms and soles of the feet. Rebalancing the cyclic AMP/GMP ratio is a prime therapeutic goal in the relief of psoriasis.

Many research scientists and specialists consider psoriasis to be one of the more than one hundred types of arthritis. Between 15 and 30 percent of people with psoriasis develop other symptoms of arthritis.[7] One theory is that psoriasis develops too many T cells. It is suspected that this overreaction of the immune system may be caused by certain drugs, hormonal changes, smoking, climate changes or infection.

There are a large number of factors that appear to be responsible for the problems associated with psoriasis. Some of these include bowel toxemia, incomplete protein digestion, alcohol consumption, excessive consumption of animal fats and impaired liver function.

Cleansing and correcting abnormal liver function is of tremendous benefit in the treatment of psoriasis. There is a strong connection between psoriasis and the liver that relates to the liver's basic task of cleansing and filtering the blood. Psoriasis has been linked to several microbial by-products, and whenever the liver is overwhelmed by increased numbers of these toxins, or if there is a decrease in the liver's ability to filter these toxins, then the level of these compounds circulating in the blood is increased. Psoriasis then becomes much worse.

Our liver can become absolutely overwhelmed with our toxic environment in our modern-day lifestyles. Alcohol consumption also is known to worsen psoriasis, as it puts a considerably heavier load on the liver to filter out the poisons. Also, alcohol's negative effects are the result of increasing the absorption of toxins from the gut, along with severely impairing liver function. An absolute must for psoriasis patients is to eliminate alcohol completely.

Special considerations for skin disease

Thankfully, God does not intend for you to suffer from any type of skin disorder. His desire is for you to be healthy, prosperous and pain free. (See 3 John 2.) As you begin to apply the following proven protocol to your skin disorder, take a moment to prepare yourself mentally, emotionally and especially spiritually. Review the prayer and scripture at the beginning of this chapter. And know that I am praying for your healing, as well.

The natural approach. Skin brushing and using mesh scrubs in the bath and shower will assist in keeping the skin clean and the pores open for efficient elimination. Benefits may also be realized from healthy massage oils (olive), fresh air, sunlight, mineral baths, and hot and cold showers. The liver and kidneys need to be cleansed of impurities, which can be accomplished through eating the correct foods and using healing herbs. Selected herbs and juices, as well as fasting, will help to keep the blood clean. Cleansing the lower bowel with selected foods and herbs is always helpful. Exercise is beneficial as well for lymphatic cleansing and eliminating toxins.

Foods to consider for healing. Raw fruit and veggies are cleansing and are packed with vitamins and minerals. Consume green salads regularly—remember the darker the greens, the more packed with nutrients. Carrots and carrot juice provide beta carotene, one of the essentials for skin health. Brown rice will help to retain nutrients for nourishing and healing the skin. Other healing veggies that should be consumed in quantity are green and red peppers, mustard greens, collard greens and turnip greens.

> As for God, his way is perfect. All the LORD's promises prove true.
> —2 Samuel 22:31, NLT

Vitamins, minerals and herbs. Vitamins A and D work together synergistically for skin health. The B-complex vitamins, with emphasis on B_2, B_6 and niacin, are also strongly recommended. Vitamin E can be taken orally and also applied externally for additional help in healing the skin. Potassium, manganese, calcium, magnesium, selenium and zinc working together synergistically are very beneficial for the skin.

Herbs that can help cleanse and strengthen the immune system include goldenseal, red clover, echinacea, fenugreek and pau d'arco. Aloe vera and comfrey also heal and build cells. Chaparral and capsicum clean out toxins and cleanse the liver.

The miracle nutrients. Lecithin, aloe vera juice and salmon oil are extremely helpful in healing skin conditions. As with other degenerative diseases, organic apple cider vinegar and oil of oregano are also extremely healing. Simply add 1 tablespoon of apple cider vinegar to your favorite juice each morning. An adequate dosage for oil of oregano is 10 to 20 drops under your tongue, adjusted as needed.

The extracts of bitter melon or balsam pear are very effective in lowering the levels of cyclic GMP and have been shown to inhibit the rapid proliferation of skin cells described above. The amino acid cysteine also reduces cyclic GMP levels, and antioxidants suppress free radical-induced elevations in cyclic GMP. Also, zinc seems particularly helpful due to its anti-inflammatory effects. Finally, glutathione, selenium and vitamin E in a synergistic formula have proven to be extremely helpful with psoriasis patients.

Taking flaxseed, sunflower seeds, almonds and cashews, consuming a variety of beans and lentils, especially black beans, and exposing the skin to twenty or thirty minutes of sunshine on a daily basis have proven to be very effective therapy for psoriasis, as well.

Spiritual assistance

You will find an abundance of inspiration and assistance in God's Holy Word. As you spend time reading the Bible, you will find the enlightening words you need to be inspired for the task ahead. Ask God for help and strength, and you can be assured that He will hear you and answer your prayers according to His will. And it is His will for you to enjoy health according to the Scriptures. (See 3 John 2.)

Living in health will enable you to serve God and others, lifting His name up so that people will be drawn to God's love through you. When you are whole again, you will be able to better serve this divine purpose. Know also, that I am praying for your complete healing, for renewed total health for you in body, mind and spirit. And consider the following wonderful promises:

> But in my distress I cried out to the LORD; yes, I called to my God for help. He heard me from his sanctuary; my cry reached his ears...He reached down from heaven and rescued me; he drew me out of deep waters...He led me to a place of safety; he rescued me because he delights in me...O LORD, you are my light; yes, LORD, you light up my darkness. In your strength I can crush an army; with my God I can scale any wall. As for God, his way is perfect. All the LORD's promises prove true.
>
> —*2 Samuel 22:7, 17, 20, 29–31, NLT*

> The more you grow like this, the more you will become productive and useful in your knowledge of our Lord Jesus Christ.
>
> —*2 Peter 1:8, NLT*

A prayer for your healing pathway from God

Heavenly Father, I realize that You have already given me the power and discipline to use the protocol given to me in this book to overcome psoriasis or scleroderma. (See 2 Timothy 1:7.) Help me now to use it. Thank You for the increased capacity I will have to serve You and others as a result of being well. I will give You the glory for how You will heal me and work through me to draw others to You. Amen.

ARTHRITIS

Arthritis is generally defined as inflammation of a joint, usually accompanied by pain, swelling and sometimes a change in body structure. It is sometimes associated with infection, rheumatic fever, trauma and various other conditions.

There are over one hundred identified forms of arthritis, including gout and bursitis.[8] Various forms may affect the lungs, spleen, blood vessels, muscles and skin (including scleroderma). Some forms of arthritis are caused by calcium deposits and deposits of uric acid in the joints, such as gout that appears around the ankles. Evidence exists pointing to the fact that some forms of arthritis may be related to allergies.

When a weakened, confused immune system attacks, white blood cells flood the tissue that lines the joint, resulting in heat and swelling. The lining begins to grow abnormally as inflammation lingers, and this causes an invasion of the bone and cartilage in the area; it also affects the muscle and connective tissue (ligaments and tendons). Eventually the joint can become deformed, weak and painful.

Arthritis appears to be aggravated by the compounding, accumulating effect of toxic wastes in the body. It is an acidic body, resulting from toxicity, that allows degenerative disease to begin and advance in the body.

Finally, arthritic tendencies appear to be inherited.

Rheumatoid arthritis

This challenging degenerative disease is one of the most difficult to deal with as far as slowing or reversing the process once it has started. Rheumatoid arthritis and osteoarthritis both cause joint pain as well as stiffness and swelling. However, this is where the similarities between the two diseases end. Rheumatoid arthritis is rather unique in that its development is usually symmetrical, meaning that it affects the joints in a mirror fashion on either side of the body. Most often it settles in the finger and wrist joints, although it can affect other parts of the body, and is usually accompanied by fever, tiredness and a general flu-like feeling.

Osteoarthritis

Osteoarthritis is an aging, wearing-away, degenerative condition. Cartilage in the joints wastes away, and calcium spurs may form on surfaces as a result of bone on bone contact. Some risk factors involved are aging, obesity, trauma and overuse or abuse of joints from sports activities or strenuous occupations.

There are natural ways to treat the various forms of arthritis that can bring relief and healing, and thankfully God has provided this natural approach so that you do not have to suffer from the pain of arthritis. When you feel better, you are able to serve Him and others better.

Special considerations for arthritis

So now take a moment to prepare yourself mentally, emotionally and spiritually as you begin your healing pathway. Look back to the prayer and scripture at the beginning of this chapter for guidance and encouragement. And remember, it is also my prayer that this proven protocol will bring you to healing. Carefully consider the following guidelines that can bring healing to your body, mind and spirit.

The natural approach. The body becomes very acidic with these arthritic conditions, causing the cartilage to deteriorate because of the acid in the blood and joints. As a result, the alkaline diet is quite effective in helping to correct this condition. Drink distilled water and use cleansing diets such as my Twenty-one-Day Detoxification Program, which calls for alkaline foods. Also see the information on pH balancing at the beginning of this chapter. Juice fasting (especially with fresh celery and carrot juice) one day a week can be very helpful.

Foods to consider for healing. Consider fresh fruits and veggies, either raw or lightly steamed. Other foods to include in the diet are green salads, squash, onions, garlic, cabbage, brown rice, millet, okra, celery and whole grains. Fresh vegetable juices, fresh cherries and cherry juice are especially healing and help to eliminate uric acid.

Vitamins, minerals and herbs. Vitamins, minerals and herbs used to treat the musculoskeletal, circulatory, nervous and digestive systems are most beneficial. Magnesium, calcium, vitamin E, selenium, zinc, manganese, the B-complex vitamins (B_6, B_{12}, niacin and pantothenic acid) and vitamin A are especially effective in a synergistic formula.

Some herbs that are helpful are red clover and white willow for pain, aloe vera and burdock to assist with utilizing oils, and kelp, which is rich in minerals for healing.

Alfalfa also helps with the pain, and its mineral content performs the critically important function of helping to maintain the proper acid/alkaline balance in the body. It is a fact that disease cannot manifest itself and progress in an alkaline body with a strong immune system.

The miracle nutrients. Distilled water, green drinks (such as spirulina, blue-green algae, wheat grass and barley grass), coenzyme Q_{10}, rice bran extract, tea tree oil, organic apple cider vinegar and lecithin are all very effective cleansing and nourishing miracle nutrients that will enhance the healing process. Essiac tea, which contains organic burdock root, organic sheep sorrel, slippery elm bark and organic turkey rhubarb, is one of the most powerful total body cleansers for aiding systemic conditions. Finally, a powerful miracle nutrient with an amazing capacity for clearing toxins and cleansing is oil of oregano. An adequate dosage is 10 to 20 drops under your tongue daily, adjusted as needed.

The omega-6 fatty acids are especially helpful in relieving the pain and swelling of arthritis. One of the omega-6 fatty acids that is most effective is gamma linoleic acid (GLA). Some good sources of GLA are evening primrose oil and black currant. Another essential fatty acid (EFA) to consider comes from the omega-3 family and is found in flaxseed. This EFA is extremely effective for relieving the pain and the swelling associated with all forms of arthritis.

Fish oil is another form of omega-3 fatty acid that works well. The good news here is when the fish oil is used in bulk, there is a significant decrease in the pain and swelling of all forms of arthritis, which can drastically reduce the need for drug therapy. Consider pantothenic acid (vitamin B_5) as a B-complex vitamin that dramatically reduces the pain and inflammation of arthritis. This is truly a wonder natural acid because it does for your joints what cortisone does and without the horrible side effects of the steroid.

Finally, be certain that you take a very potent multivitamin on a daily basis.

Spiritual assistance

God's Word is loaded with promises to inspire and uplift you. Look to His Word continually, for He has promised never to leave you or forsake you. (See Deuteronomy 4:31.) Draw strength from His promises so that you will be successful and prosperous. (See Joshua 1:8.) And know that He delights in answering your prayer to Him. You have a need for the strength and discipline that only God can give you as you begin this great endeavor to make lifestyle choices consistently that will bring healing to your body. Consider these wonderful promises:

> For he has not despised or disdained the suffering of the afflicted one; he has not hidden his face from him but listened to his cry for help.
>
> —*Psalm 22:24, NIV*

> O Lord, you are my God; I will exalt you and praise your name, for in perfect faithfulness you have done marvelous things, things planned long ago.
>
> —*Isaiah 25:1, NIV*

A prayer for your healing pathway from God

> *Heavenly Father, thank You for the power and discipline You have already given me to utilize the anointed protocol in this book to overcome arthritis. (See 2 Timothy 1:7.) Please help me draw upon that power and discipline. And as I become well, help me to be more aware of the perfect plan You have for my life. Allow me, because of my new strength and wellness, to better serve You and others. And I will give You the glory. Amen.*

AIDS (ACQUIRED IMMUNE DEFICIENCY SYNDROME)

The immune system is completely dismantled by AIDS, which is caused by a virus and is complicated by other disorders. These disorders usually accompany AIDS because, with a destroyed immune system, the body is totally vulnerable to whatever is contracted.

Dr. Eva Snead's book *Some Call It AIDS—I Call It Murder* reveals her research that asserts that the AIDS virus was developed in a laboratory in Africa from the kidney of the African green monkey.[9] She believes that the World Health Organization was responsible for initializing the AIDS epidemic with their smallpox immunization campaign. Almost 100 million people were vaccinated in Africa. Some reports estimated that one-third of the total African population would have the disease by 2003. Dr. William Douglass in his book *AIDS: The End of Civilization,* stated that this represented the greatest biological disaster in the history of man.[10]

You need to accept the fact that God does want you to be healthy. Look to the prayer and scripture at the beginning of this chapter to help prepare yourself mentally, emotionally and spiritually for your battle against AIDS. Do not underestimate God's healing power—the power that results from restoring the body's immune system through natural therapy along with prayer and petition to Him. And do not be afraid, for the Lord your God is with you wherever you go. (See Joshua 1:9.)

Special considerations for AIDS

Let's now take a look at the specific ways you can boost your body's immune system, which will help you in your battle to overcome AIDS.

A natural approach. While we cannot overestimate the difficulty of reversing the devastating effects of the AIDS virus on the body, we do offer hope that restoring the body's damaged immune system can strengthen its innate ability to deal with even the most vicious disease. The comprehensive protocol outlined in this book for rebuilding the body's defenses can prove helpful to prevent, as well as reverse, symptoms of AIDS along with other serious degenerative diseases it has been proven to help.

Foods to consider for healing. The foods most effective in assisting to heal the body and strengthen the immune system are raw fruits and vegetables, especially those that are extremely high in vitamins A and C. These include yellow vegetables, citrus fruits, strawberries, alfalfa sprouts, papaya, kale, parsley, broccoli, wheat grass and barley grass.

Cabbage, turnips, squash, garlic and onions are also helpful for the cleansing and boosting of the immune system. Brown rice, millet or buckwheat, cooked in a thermos (which will help to retain the enzymes for proper digestion), are extremely helpful. Beans and sprouted grains will also help to supply needed nutrients.

Vitamins, minerals and herbs. The antioxidant vitamins and minerals that are greatly needed are vitamins A, C, D and E, along with the powerful micro-mineral antioxidants selenium and zinc. B-complex vitamins are also needed for brain and nervous system health, as well as for good digestion. Magnesium, calcium, potassium and chromium are also extremely vital for boosting the immune system so that it can become more efficient in attacking this devastating virus.

Some of the more effective herbs for improving the immune system are gingko, goldenseal, licorice, kelp, bee pollen, burdock, echinacea, garlic, suma and psyllium.

The miracle nutrients. Whereas candida is a most common condition with AIDS, acidophilus is a much-needed nutrient. Blue-green algae and chlorophyll possess very effective and powerful natural antibiotic properties and are especially high in vitamin A and beta carotene. Coenzyme Q_{10} is especially needed to provide oxygen for the blood and to assist in keeping the heart and the arteries healthy. Finally, salmon oil, lecithin and flaxseed are valuable in strengthening the immune system.

A powerful multimineral to promote the enhancement of the production of all the major hormones, including the human growth hormone, is extremely beneficial.

Spiritual assistance

Now more than ever, you will find help, strength and comfort in God's Word. He has promised to never abandon you, no matter how discouraged you may be. Claim His promises. He *will* give you strength to fight this disease. And I am praying for you as well— praying for you to be uplifted and for your immune system to be strengthened as you follow this protocol and look to God and His promises for power. Others have found help in God as the Scriptures record:

> I waited patiently for the LORD; and He inclined to me, and heard my cry. He also brought me up out of a horrible pit, out of the miry clay, and set my feet upon a rock, and established my steps.
>
> —*Psalm 40:1–2*

> And the Holy Spirit helps us in our distress. For we don't even know what we should pray for, nor how we should pray. But the Holy Spirit prays for us with groanings that cannot be expressed in words. And the Father who knows

all hearts knows what the Spirit is saying, for the Spirit pleads for us believers in harmony with God's own will. And we know that God causes everything to work together for the good of those who love God and are called according to his purpose for them.

—Romans 8:26–28, NLT

A prayer for your healing pathway from God

Heavenly Father, I claim Your promise that the Holy Spirit will intercede for me, and I thank You that He prays for me with groanings that cannot be expressed in words. I know You have already given me the power and the discipline to use the protocol in this book for strengthening my immune system. (See 2 Timothy 1:7.) Now strengthen me to apply it. I thank You now for the healing that will take place and for my renewed strength. I know that I will better be able to serve You and others as I feel better, and I thank You for the opportunity I will have to do so as a result of my being stronger. And I will give You the glory for the work you will do. Amen.

CANCER

The primary causes of cancer are stress and trauma factors, poor nutrition and exercise habits, and environmental toxin accumulations, which taken together result in a compromised immune system and toxicity of the body. This weakened condition of the systems of the body allows normal cells to get out of control, which can trigger the growth and progression of "free radicals," the precursors to cancer cells.

Food additives and preservatives, air and water impurities, heavy metals, agricultural chemical exposure, household chemicals and excessive prescription drug use all contribute to a dangerous vulnerability to cancer. Due to these factors, we are all at risk to some degree and face a tremendous challenge in the attempt to stay well. These facts reinforce the increased need for everyone to pursue the healthful lifestyle outlined in the protocol described in this book.

As you know, there are numerous types of cancer that can attack various parts of the body, including the skin, muscles, internal organs or lymphatic system. Cancer is a serious disorder of the immune system, causing cells to malfunction. Malignancy is defined as cancer cells that are stimulated to reproduce and invade other parts of the body. If not controlled or stopped, cancer cells that form tumors even grow their own blood vessels in order to spread their deadly malignancy.

Thankfully, our heavenly Father does not intend for you to suffer from cancer or any other disease. His desire is for you to be healthy and prosperous. (See 3 John 2.) God wants to give you back your health, but you need to commit to a plan of action that has proven successful. (See Jeremiah 30:17.) The protocol you are about to read is one of those plans of action. Together with your determination and the strength you draw from God, you may be able to prevent the growth and even reverse the effects of cancerous cells.

Before you continue, take a moment to review the prayer and scripture at the beginning of this chapter. And know that I am praying for you as well—praying that your total health will be restored so that you may accomplish the purpose that God has for you. Consider this wonderful promise:

> But the godly will flourish like palm trees and grow strong like the cedars of Lebanon. For they are transplanted into the LORD's own house. They flourish in the courts of our God. Even in old age they will still produce fruit; they will remain vital and green.
>
> —*Psalm 92:12–14*, NLT

Take comfort in knowing that God's plan for you is to enjoy your old age.

Special considerations for cancer

Because cancer is a result of a general weakening of our immune system and overall health, as we discussed, it is extremely beneficial to commit to major lifestyle changes such as the protocol I have outlined in this book. Since there is no magic bullet cure for this disease, there is a definite need to combine synergistically all of the areas relating to health that we have discussed.

It has been firmly established that the primary cause of cancer is the presence of poisons and toxins in the bloodstream. A cancer or tumor is an indication that the blood and the liver have become overloaded and are unable to eliminate in the normal way because of constipation and autointoxication. Therefore, the growth of cancer cells is triggered within our system.

Cancer is much more common today because of the greater abundance of toxins in our food, water and air. Fast foods, additives, fillers and so many preservatives in processed foods are some of the primary problems. When junk food is consistently consumed, along with our poor lifestyles, our cells become toxic and/or inefficient in eliminating toxins. A subsequent accumulation of these toxins results in contamination of tissues, and cancers and tumors soon follow. It is apparent, then, that excellent nutrition, supplementation and detoxification will speed up the elimination of toxins, which destroy organs that build and clean the blood.

The natural approach. Using natural therapies to strengthen the immune system is of essence for combating cancer. The Centers for Disease Control in Atlanta, Georgia, has released information confirming the connection between cancer and diet, which has become commonly accepted during the last few years. Blood, liver and body cleansing should get particular attention on a regular basis. (See chapter five for more detailed information.)

Foods to consider for healing. High-fiber diets including beans, bean sprouts, lentils, whole grains, oatmeal, brown rice and buckwheat are necessary for giving the body adequate nutrition for healing. The cruciferous vegetables are especially known to help protect against cancer. Some of these to consider are broccoli, brussels sprouts, cauliflower, cabbage, turnips, kale and mustard greens. These vegetables contain helpful health compounds called indole-3-carbinols that disarm estrogen and prevent the cancerous growth process, especially in breast cancer.

Other food sources that are helpful are almonds, barley juice, wheat grass juice, flaxseed, sunflower seeds, cherries, carrots (for beta carotene) and all raw fruits and vegetables. Be sure to review the general nutritional considerations listed at the beginning of this chapter, which are important for fighting all types of degenerative disease and maintaining proper health.

Cancer patients should avoid meat because it is simply dead matter that is very low in minerals and produces uric acid, which is harmful to the blood and can cause other problems. Also, eliminate salt-cured, salt-pickled and smoked foods such as bacon, ham, sausage and bologna. Eliminate bad fats, and all of these recommendations together will help to prevent constipation and the accumulation of foreign substances in the body, which is basically the main cause of all disease.

Vitamins, minerals and herbs. Vitamins A, C, D and E are very effective antioxidants for combating cancer. Antioxidants work to destroy and neutralize harmful toxins and buffer harmful substances that are cancer-causing agents. It is essential to take a multivitamin daily with extra calcium, manganese, magnesium, selenium and zinc. Vitamin D also helps by aiding the body in utilizing minerals, vitamin A, calcium and magnesium.

Herbs that are very important for cancer prevention and reversal are garlic and echinacea (natural antibiotics) and red clover and capsicum (liver and blood cleansers). Pau d'arco is extremely potent as a total body and blood cleanser also.

Fresh juice fasting, barley grass, wheat grass, blue-green algae and chlorella help to inhibit and destroy cancer cells. Alfalfa also contains anti-cancer properties. Other herbs that are extremely helpful with protection are aloe vera, bee pollen, black walnuts, goldenseal, kelp and horsetail.

The miracle nutrients. The green drink that includes barley grass, wheat grass, spirulina, blue-green algae and flaxseed, discussed in the detoxification chapter, is excellent for normalizing cell growth. Salmon oil, liquid chlorophyll, evening primrose oil and echinacea herbal tea are all special agents for the immune system.

Organic apple cider vinegar is especially effective for clearing toxins; it has a double punch when mixed with organic apple cider. The apple cider contains malic acid, which combines with magnesium to nourish body tissues and refurbish the energy cycle. Add 1 tablespoon of the vinegar to apple cider each morning. Also, oil of oregano cleanses and removes toxins. Try 10 to 20 drops under your tongue to begin with, then adjust as needed.

Camas prairie tea (better known as Essiac tea) is also known for its effectiveness with cancer patients.

Spiritual assistance

Find comfort, strength and assistance in God's Word. You will need all of this help as you determine to make significant changes in your lifestyle and begin to reverse or prevent the effects of cancer. God has promised to be there for you in your time of need; He will never leave you or forsake you. (See Deuteronomy 4:31.) Call out to Him and expect Him to hear you and answer your calls for strength as you make lasting changes in your health by following this protocol.

As you become healthy, you will be able to better serve God and others, and you will have a greater understanding and appreciation of what God's purpose is for you. Remember, as you feel better, you will be more effective in serving Him, in lifting Him up so that others may be drawn to Him through you. Consider these wonderful promises:

> The LORD is righteous in everything he does; he is filled with kindness. The LORD is close to all who call on him, yes, to all who call on him sincerely. He fulfills the desires of those who fear him; he hears their cries for help and rescues them.
>
> *—Psalm 145:17–19,* NLT

> The more you grow like this, the more you will become productive and useful in your knowledge of our Lord Jesus Christ.
>
> *—2 Peter 1:8*

A prayer for your healing pathway from God

> *Heavenly Father, thank You for the power and discipline You have already given me to use this protocol to prevent and overcome cancer. (See 2 Timothy 1:7.) I ask You now for strength, and I praise You for the purpose for which You created me—to commune with You and share You with others. As I become healthier, help me to understand fully this purpose so that I will better serve You and others. And I will give You the glory forever. Amen.*

CONCLUSION

I would like to challenge and encourage you to embark on your new venture toward wholeness and wellness with confidence, discipline and faith in God. Remember, I shared with you earlier that literally hundreds around the globe have experienced relief and recovery after following my protocol.

It should be extremely exciting to you to think that no matter what your condition, you can return to health and vitality. Don't fret if your particular condition is not listed here. Remember, no matter what your condition or disease, this protocol is effective in assisting the body to correct it because the protocol is based on health principles that allow the body to be restored to health.

If you will make a firm commitment and ask God to help you exercise a focused discipline, you will return to vibrant health and be all that God intended you to be. Your Creator's greatest desire is that you be healthy and prosper as your soul prospers. (See 3 John 2.)

It is my heart's desire that you find God's pathway for you in your venture back to wholeness and wellness. My prayer is that this book will be a blessing to your life and health. May God bless you and yours as you seek wellness and determine to live a healthy lifestyle to fulfill the purpose of God for your life.

As you achieve success in returning to vital health, I would love to hear your success story. Please feel free to contact my office and share your story with us. We covenant with you in prayer and faith for your healing, health and happiness. Whenever possible, share your medical history and/or records with us before beginning the program and after you achieve your goals for wellness. I look forward to publishing an entire book filled with success stories sharing with other hurting people how you got your health and life back.

God bless and speed you toward healing and wholeness.

Part IV

Dr. Elrod's Twelve-Week Protocol

DR. ELROD'S TWELVE-WEEK
BODY ADVANTAGE PROTOCOL

As you prepare to complete my twelve-week protocol, specific instructions and samples of forms that you can use to log your progress are included for the three phases of the program.

I have prepared a complete workbook that contains all of the forms needed, which you can obtain if desired, along with a video and exercise device for strength exercises. Please refer to the product page for ordering these materials. Otherwise, you may copy the forms included here to have one for each week of the program in order to log your daily activities and follow your progress through:

Phase I: Weeks 1–4

Phase II: Weeks 5–8

Phase III: Weeks 9–12

CHAPTER 11

Phase I: Balancing

Here are some tips for getting started with lifestyle changes that are doable:

PROTOCOL GUIDELINES

- Adjust eating patterns gradually.

- Progress at your own pace as sleep and energy levels begin to improve.

- Educate your loved ones about this program so that they may support you in your efforts (and may even decide to improve their health and start the program with you).

- Involve your spouse in making some of these changes with you, such as improving the sleeping environment, reducing stress and adjusting eating patterns.

- Get an exercise partner, and motivate each other to stick with an exercise routine.

- Carry water bottles with you at all times.

- Plan meals; use a list when grocery shopping.

- Chop and prepare veggies ahead of time so that they are available at all times.

- Keep a journal and complete the forms and work-sheets in this book.

- While learning new behavior patterns, review your goals daily.

- Review the Phase I Completion Checklist on page 200 frequently to be sure you are on track with your goals.

GETTING STARTED CHECKLIST

The following checklist is to determine if you fully understand the steps of The Body Advantage Program and if you now feel prepared to accomplish your goals.

I have:	Yes	No
Received clearance from my physician to begin my Body Advantage Program.	☐	☐
Started drinking a minimum of three 20-ounce bottles of water daily.	☐	☐
Adjusted my daily schedule to allow for my healthy lifestyle.	☐	☐
Considered my goals for Phase I and feel confident that I can accomplish them. (See Goals Worksheet on page 196.)	☐	☐
Responded to the Attitude Assessment Questionnaire on page 29.	☐	☐
Shared my goals with friends and family so that I will be more accountable for accomplishing them.	☐	☐
Read and signed The Body Advantage Wellness Contract on page 39.	☐	☐

PHASE I TASKS

Commitment

Commit to the Twenty-one-Day Detoxification Program by establishing a date to begin:

- I will begin the ten-day tapering period on
  _____.

- I will begin the Twenty-one-Day Detoxification
  program on _____.

Your personal commitment to make some lifestyle changes for health should bring a sense of hope and expectation, even joy, to your heart and mind. My goal is to help eliminate doubts and questions that may arise concerning whether or not you will succeed in your efforts.

As you continue, please allow your mind and heart to relax and contemplate the days ahead when you will be feeling much healthier and enjoying life from the perspective of health. Your program begins here, with a focus on ways to de-stress your life to set the stage for a healthier lifestyle.

Exercise guidelines

- If you have been inactive, you will begin with Phase I exercises only.

- If somewhat active, you may decide to begin with Phase II exercises.

- If very active and fit physically, you may even add some alternative activities in Phase III.

Goals

Complete the goals listed in the Phase I Goals worksheet.

PHASE I GOALS: WEEKS 1–4

During the next four weeks of Phase I, you will be gradually introducing all six steps to health into your lifestyle by choosing to make lifestyle changes for health. Set your own goals for this important new beginning, and enjoy the progress you make. Don't be discouraged if they are not done perfectly; just continue to incorporate them into your lifestyle.

GOALS WORKSHEET

Step 1: Stress Management

Choose three items from the list of tools for stress reduction (pages 48–49, 52) to work on:

1.

2.

3.

Step 2: Detoxification

During Phase I, you should:

1. Do the Twenty-one-Day Detoxification Program.

2. Drink 60 ounces of water daily.

3. Use litmus strips to monitor and balance pH.

Step 3: Eat for Life

During Phase I:

1. Read chapter six several times for understanding the nutritional principles.

2. Begin to plan shopping, meals and snacks ahead of time.

3. Begin to develop your routine of meals, snacks and water, and logging your progress in your planning charts.

4. Begin to reduce alcohol, caffeine and sugar consumption.

Step 4: Supplement for Efficiency

Be sure to review chapter seven to understand the importance of taking vitamins and minerals. Aim to begin supplementing with a quality multivitamin and mineral, if you are not already doing so. Then refer to the section on miracle nutrients and see which of those you want to try that apply to your condition.

Be sure to include your physician in your decisions, especially if you are taking medications, since some herbs and nutrients can interact with medications in a negative way.

Step 5: The Power of Exercise

Choose your level of activity from the exercise protocol in Phase I, Phase II or Phase III, depending on your evaluation of where you fit best at present. Do not overestimate your physical fitness; it is better to begin below your present level than to push your body too hard in the beginning.

Exercise protocol: Phase 1

- Stretching—one set of basic stretches two days a week. (See pages 116–119 for suggested exercises.)

- Aerobic—sixty aerobic minutes per week. (Complete four fifteen-minute sessions minimum.)

- Strength—one set of basic exercises two days a week. (See pages 121–129 for strength-training instructions, or use The Body Advantage Exercise System complete with video instructions.)

Step 6: Restoring Deep Sleep

Choose three items from the Ways to Improve Sleep section on pages 142–143 to begin adding to your lifestyle during the next four weeks:

1.

2

3.

FORMS FOR PHASE I

You may copy the following sample forms to use for each of the four weeks during Phase I. They will help you keep track of your progress as you log your activity in each of the areas of exercise, water consumption, meal planning and taking your supplements.

WEEKLY TASK PLANNER: PHASE I

	Basic Exercises (one set)	Aerobic Minutes*	Water (three 20-oz. bottles)	Three Meals and Three Snacks	Taking Supplements	Comments
Monday						
Tuesday						
Wednesday						
Thursday						
Friday						
Saturday						
Sunday						
Totals/Week						
Goals/Week	2 days	60	3/day	6/day		

* Fifteen minutes minimum per session

WEEKLY MEAL PLANNER: PHASE I

	Breakfast	Snack	Lunch	Snack	Dinner	Snack
Monday						
Tuesday						
Wednesday						
Thursday						
Friday						
Saturday						
Sunday						

PHASE I COMPLETION CHECKLIST

Check *yes* or *no* for each question. Make notes as you think about your answer and the healthy adjustments you would like to make for each.

Yes No

I now understand my attitudes, habit patterns and ☐ ☐
emotions that affect my ability to be successful in all
areas of my life.

Adjustments: _____

_____

Yes No

My personal fitness has improved, I am moving more, ☐ ☐
and my flexibility has increased.

Adjustments: _____

_____

Yes No

I take a brisk twenty-minute walk three times a week. ☐ ☐

Adjustments: _____

_____

Yes No

I drink three 20-ounce bottles of water daily and ☐ ☐
understand the value of proper hydration.

Adjustments: _____

_____

Yes No

I have made two or three adjustments to improve deep ☐ ☐
sleep for health and healing.

Adjustments:

_____

	Yes	**No**
I successfully completed the Twenty-one-Day Detoxification Program.	☐	☐

Adjustments:

_____

	Yes	**No**
I understand The Body Advantage Nutrition Protocol. I have adjusted my schedule, changed the way I shop, adjusted my eating patterns and eat six smaller, healthier meals daily.	☐	☐

Adjustments:

_____

	Yes	**No**
I have developed a schedule and consistently take my supplements.	☐	☐

Adjustments:

_____

	Yes	**No**
I am prepared mentally, emotionally and physically for the next phase of The Body Advantage Program and a lifetime of health and fitness.	☐	☐

Adjustments:

_____

CHAPTER 12

Phase II: Progressing

Congratulations! You have completed the first four weeks of the program and are ready to progress to Phase II. Do not be discouraged if you did not do everything perfectly every day. Remember, these are gradual lifestyle adjustments that will become habits to help you restore and maintain health for the rest of your life. Here are the guidelines for Phase II to keep you moving toward a healthy lifestyle.

PROTOCOL GUIDELINES

- Continue eating pattern adjustments.

- Expand your exercise regimen. You should have an established stretching routine by now; consider doing your own regimen twice per day.

- Continue supplementing your nutritional plan with vitamins, minerals and other miracle nutrients. You will need to consider the most economical and effective way to continue proper supplementation for life. (See chapter seven for instructions.)

- Continue to add to your positive sleep habit patterns—you should have made several adjustments by now. (See chapter nine.)

- Take a look at stress management adjustments you have made and consider what else needs to be done.

- Reaffirm your Body Advantage Wellness Contract.

- Look back at the attitude and habit pattern changes you started to work on in Phase I. Evaluate your progress and commit to continue working on your positive attitude and stress management skills.

- Review your information on hydration, and then evaluate your progress on consuming adequate amounts of water.

- You should be ready to move forward and progress mentally, emotionally and physically.

PHASE II GOALS: WEEKS 5–8

Here are the specific goals for the second four-week period of the program:

- Increase water to four 20-ounce bottles per day.

- Increase your strength exercise routine to two sets twice a week.

- Increase aerobic activity to eighty minutes a week.

- Maintain your supplement regimen—check them off daily.

- Continue to limit alcohol and caffeine consumption.

- Maintain your exercise and food charts.

- Work to understand the cause of emotional eating, and then eliminate it.

- Make two or three new adjustments to improve sleep.

- Make two or three new adjustments to improve stress management skills.

GOALS WORKSHEET

Step 1: Stress Management

Choose three new items from the list of tools for stress reduction (pages 48–49, 52) to work on:

1.

2.

3.

Step 2: Detoxification

During Phase II, you should do the following:

1. Increase water consumption to 80 ounces of water daily.

2. Use litmus strips to monitor and balance pH.

Step 3: Eat for Life

During Phase II continue to improve nutrition habits. You may find it helpful to do the following:

1. Continue to add new, wholesome foods to your diet.

2. Decrease alcohol, caffeine and sugar consumption further.

3. Visit a health food store and become aware of what is available to you.

Step 4: Supplement for Efficiency

Continue the supplements you began in Phase I, and read again the chapter on supplementation (chapter seven) to see what other nutrients you may need.

Experiment with new flavors of teas and with other miracle nutrients that may apply to your condition.

Step 5: The Power of Exercise

Advance to the next level of activity from the following exercise protocol. List your selected exercises below:

1. Stretching:

2. Aerobics:

3. Strength:

Exercise protocol: Phase II

- Stretching—increase basic stretches to three days a week.

- Aerobic—increase aerobic activity to eighty aerobic minutes per week (four twenty-minute sessions minimum).

- Strength—increase to two sets of basic exercises two days a week. (See pages 121–129 for strength-training instructions, or use The Body Advantage Exercise System complete with video instructions.)

Step 6: Restoring Deep Sleep

Choose three new items from the Ways to Improve Sleep section on pages 142–143 to begin adding to your lifestyle during the next four weeks.

1.

2.

3.

FORMS FOR PHASE II

You may copy the following sample forms to use for each of the four weeks during Phase II. They will continue to help you keep track of your progress as you log your activity in each of the areas of exercise, water consumption, meal planning and taking your supplements.

WEEKLY TASK PLANNER: PHASE II

	Basic Exercises (one set)	Aerobic Minutes*	Water (four 20-oz. bottles)	Three Meals and Three Snacks	Taking Supplements	Comments
Monday						
Tuesday						
Wednesday						
Thursday						
Friday						
Saturday						
Sunday						
Totals/Week						
Goals/Week	3 days	80	4/day	6/day		

* Twenty minutes minimum per session

WEEKLY MEAL PLANNER: PHASE II

	Breakfast	Snack	Lunch	Snack	Dinner	Snack
Monday						
Tuesday						
Wednesday						
Thursday						
Friday						
Saturday						
Sunday						

CHAPTER 13

Phase III: Maintaining

Congratulations! You have completed eight weeks of the program and are ready to progress to Phase III. Again, you probably did not do everything perfectly every day. But I predict you are feeling better physically and have more of a sense of well-being. Your outlook on life should be brighter just because you are working at your commitment to make a difference in your lifestyle that will impact your health positively.

As you begin the last four weeks of my twelve-week program, remember that you are not anticipating returning to the unhealthy lifestyle that damaged your health in the first place. Try to make as many permanent changes as you can, reinforcing your good behavior with healthy rewards. Here are your guidelines for Phase III.

PROTOCOL GUIDELINES

- You should be leveled out with a healthy eating pattern at this stage.

- Your exercise regimen should be complete with alternative aerobic activities added.

- Continue supplementing your nutritional plan with vitamins, minerals and other miracle nutrients.

- Positive sleep patterns should be well established— stay disciplined.

- Evaluate stress management progress and continue to sharpen these skills.

- Consistent positive attitude and healthy habit patterning should become routine.

- The healthy water issue should be a way of life.

- Remember to be cognizant of keeping it all together mentally, emotionally and physically.

PHASE III GOALS: WEEKS 9–12

Here are the specific goals for the final four weeks of the program:

- Drink four 20-ounce bottles of water daily.

- Increase strength exercises to three sets two times a week.

- Increase aerobic activity to one hundred twenty minutes a week.

- Begin to include alternative aerobic activities (for example, swimming and cycling).

- Maintain your supplement regimen.

- Continue to limit alcohol, caffeine and sugar consumption.

- Maintain your exercise and food charts.

GOALS WORKSHEET

Step 1: Stress Management

Choose three new items from the list of tools for stress reduction (pages 48–49, 52) to work on:

1.

2.

3.

Step 2: Detoxification

During Phase III, you should do the following:

1. Maintain water consumption at 80 ounces of water daily.

2. Use litmus strips to monitor and balance pH.

Step 3: Eat for Life

During Phase III, continue to improve nutrition habits. You may find it helpful to do the following:

1. Continue to add new, wholesome foods to your diet.

2. Read the chapter on nutrition again (chapter six) to make sure you are incorporating needed aspects into your regimen.

Step 4: Supplement for Efficiency

Continue the supplements you began in Phase I and any you added in Phase II. Be sure to continue to familiarize yourself with miracle nutrients that may be helpful to you.

Step 5: The Power of Exercise

Advance to the next level of activity from the following exercise protocol. List your selected exercises below.

1. Stretching:

2. Aerobics:

3. Strength:

Exercise protocol: Phase III

- Stretching—maintain basic stretches at three days a week.

- Aerobic—increase aerobic activity to one hundred twenty aerobic minutes per week (four thirty-minute sessions minimum).

- Strength—increase to three sets of basic exercises two days a week. (See pages 121–129 for strength-training instructions, or use The Body Advantage Exercise System complete with video instructions.)

Step 6: Restoring Deep Sleep

Choose three new items from the Ways to Improve Sleep section on pages 142–143 to begin adding to your lifestyle during the next four weeks:

1.

2.

3.

FORMS FOR PHASE III

Copy the following sample forms for use during each of the four weeks during Phase III. They will continue to help you keep track of your progress as you log your activity in each of the areas of exercise, water consumption, meal planning and taking your supplements.

WEEKLY TASK PLANNER: PHASE III

	Basic Exercises (one set)	Aerobic Minutes*	Water (four 20-oz. bottles)	Three Meals and Three Snacks	Taking Supplements	Comments
Monday						
Tuesday						
Wednesday						
Thursday						
Friday						
Saturday						
Sunday						
Totals/Week						
Goals/Week	3 days	120	4/day	6/day		

* Thirty minutes minimum per session

WEEKLY MEAL PLANNER: PHASE III

	Breakfast	Snack	Lunch	Snack	Dinner	Snack
Monday						
Tuesday						
Wednesday						
Thursday						
Friday						
Saturday						
Sunday						

APPENDIX

How Is Your Water Consumption?

Between 60 and 75 percent of your body makeup is water, and you lose or use large amounts of it daily through normal bodily processes. The following facts may help you reconsider your habits of water consumption:

- Most people suffer from dehydration regularly and do not know it. Their aches and pains could be relieved if they would hydrate properly.

- There is a good chance that as you read this you are behind on your water intake. Research shows that 70 to 80 percent of all people do not drink enough water. Most people are under the false impression that the many other beverages available these days adequately replace water—THEY SIMPLY DO NOT.

- If you wait until you are thirsty to drink, your thirst is your body telling you that you are dehydrated and severely behind on water intake.

- Every biological function that your body performs is compromised or impeded if you don't consume adequate amounts of water. Water is the most essential of all the nutrients we need for healthy biological functioning. Many people mistakenly don't even recognize water as a nutrient.

The following is a list of critical benefits of water for the body:

Water helps to fill your stomach.

You simply tend to eat less if you are drinking adequate amounts of water. You will also desire less caffeinated and alcoholic beverages if you are ingesting adequate amounts of water.

You tend to eat more if you are dehydrated.

Your body signals for you to eat when dehydrated; usually what you need is more water. When you are meeting your nutritional needs with a well-balanced diet and are drinking 60 to 70 ounces of water daily, you are less prone to food cravings and/or overeating.

Digestion is much more efficient when water intake is adequate.

This can have a domino effect in that when digestion is incomplete, it can prevent you from getting the needed vitamins and minerals. These deficiencies then can trigger additional eating in the body's attempt to get those missing nutrients.

You rev up your metabolism when you're taking in adequate amounts of water.

Water is the necessary component required to assist the chemical reactions necessary to burn calories both at rest and during movement.

The more active you become, the more water you need.

The normal state for the human body is to be active the major part of the day. Whenever we move, the muscles, bones, organs and connective tissues become stronger and more efficient, and more water is required. The more active you become, the more water you need. When you increase movement, you increase muscle mass, your metabolism goes up, and your need for water increases.

If you have adequate amounts of water, your exercise is more beneficial.

Active muscles not only need and store more water, but they also store more glycogen (carbohydrates needed to supply the fuel for movement). Once you begin aerobically exercising and entertaining your more active lifestyle, it will be vitally important that you consume a minimum of three 20-ounce bottles of water daily.

If you want maximum benefit from your exercise, you will want adequate amounts of water to meet the increased demands of metabolism. You will also need additional water to manage the important function of cooling your body healthfully and safely as a result of increased activity. Always make sure that you have ingested adequate amounts thirty minutes to an hour before exercise.

NOTES

CHAPTER 4
STEP 1: DE-STRESS YOUR LIFE

1. Shari Lieberman, Ph.D., C.N.S., F.A.C.N. with Nancy Bruning, *Dare to Lose: Four Simple Steps to a Better Body* (New York: Avery Publishing, 2002).

CHAPTER 5
STEP 2: DETOXIFY YOUR BODY

1. Skye Weintraub, N.D., *Natural Treatments for ADD and Hyperactivity* (Pleasant Grove, UT: Woodland Publishers, 1997).
2. D. A. Gans, "Sucrose and delinquent behavior: coincidence or consequence?" *Critical Reviews in Food and Science and Nutrition* 20 (November 1990): 2677–2678.
3. Ibid.
4. Essiac tea is a combination of organic burdock root, organic sheep sorrel, slippery elm bark and organic turkey rhubarb. It is known for its effective treatment of cancer and other ills. Essiac tea can be found in health food stores.

CHAPTER 6
STEP 3: EAT FOR LIFE

1. Joe M. Elrod, *Reversing Fibromyalgia* (Pleasant Grove, UT: Woodland Publishing, 2002), 144.
2. Jennie Brand-Miller, Ph.D. et al., *The New Glucose Revolution* (New York: Marlowe and Company, 2002).
3. C. D. Berdamier, *Advanced Nutrition: Micronutrients* (Boca Raton, FL: CRC Press, 1997).
4. C. D. Berdamier, *Desk Reference for Nutrition* (Boca Raton, FL: CRC Press, 1997).

CHAPTER 7
STEP 4: SUPPLEMENT FOR EFFICIENCY

1. R. K. Chandra, *Vitamin Deficiencies in Immunology of Nutritional Disorders* (Chicago: Yearbook Publications, 1980).
2. Weintraub, *Natural Treatments for ADD and Hyperactivity.*
3. D. E. Ballester and A. S. Prasad, "Energy, zinc deficiency and decreased nucleotide phosphorylase activity in patients with sickle cell anemia," *Ann. of Intern. Med.* (1983).
4. Deanne Tenny, *An Introduction to Natural Health* (Provo, UT: Woodland Books, 1992).
5. Ellen Mazo, ed. *The Immune Advantage* (Emmaus, PA: Rodale Press, 2002).

CHAPTER 8
STEP 5: THE POWER OF EXERCISE

1. Physical Activity Calorie Use Chart, copyright © 2002 American Heart Association, Inc. All rights reserved. Used by permission. Unauthorized use prohibited. Chart retrieved from Internet at www.americanheart.org.

CHAPTER 10
PROTOCOL FOR SPECIFIC SYSTEMIC CONDITIONS

1. D. Snowden, *Aging with Grace* (New York: Bantam, 2002).
2. H. Van Pragg et al., "Running enhances neurogenesis, learning and long-term potentiation in mice," *Proceedings of the National Academy of Sciences* (USA) 96, no. 23 (1999): 13427–13431.
3. Snowden, *Aging with Grace.*
4. Elrod, *Reversing Fibromyalgia.*
5. B. M. Calkins, A. M. Lilieneld, C. F. Garland et al., "Trends in incidence rates of ulcerative colitis and Crohn's disease," *Dig. Dis. Sci.* 29 (1984): 913–920.
6. Statistics about lupus retrieved from the Internet at www.lupus.org/education/stats.html on January 22, 2003.
7. Carolyn J. Strange, "Coping with Arthritis in Its Many Forms," *FDA Consumer* (March 1996; revised December 1996, June 1997): retrieved from the Internet on January 22, 2003 from www.fda.gov/fdac/features/296_art.html.
8. Ibid.

9. Eva Lee Snead, M.D., *Some Call It AIDS—I Call It Murder: The Connection Between Cancer, AIDS, Immunization and Genocide* (New York: Aum Publications, 1993).

10. William Campbell Douglass, M.D., *AIDS: The End of Civilization* (n.p.: A and B Book Pub. Dist., 1992).

RESOURCE LIST

American Academy of Allergy, Asthma and Immunology
611 E. Wells St.
Milwaukee, WI 53202
414-272-6071
800-822-2762

American Academy of Environmental Medicine
7701 East Kellogg, Suite 625
Wichita, KS 67207
316-684-5500
FAX: 316-684-5709

American Association for Chronic Fatigue Syndrome
515 Minor Ave., Suite 18
Seattle, WA 98104
206-781-3544
206-749-9052

American College of Rheumatology
1800 Century Place, Suite 250
Atlanta, GA 30345
404-633-3777

American Dietetic Association
216 W. Jackson Blvd.
Chicago, IL 60606-6995
312-899-0040

The Fibromyalgia Network
P. O. Box 31750
Tucson, AZ 85751-1750
800-853-2929

American Psychiatric Association, APA
1000 Wilson Blvd., Suite 1825
Arlington, VA 22209-3901
888-357-7924

American Psychological Association
750 First St., NE
Washington, DC 20002-4242
800-374-2721

Ankylosing Spondylitis Association of America
14827 Ventura Blvd., #222
Sherman Oaks, CA 91403
818-981-1616

Arthritis Foundation
P. O. Box 7669
Atlanta, GA 30357-0669
800-283-7800

The CFIDS Association of America, Inc.
P. O. Box 220398
Charlotte, NC 28222-0398
800-442-3437

Depression, Awareness, Recognition and Treatment (D/ART)
5600 Fishers Lane, Rm. 10-85
Rockville, MD 20857
800-421-4211

Food Allergy Network
4744 Holly Ave.
Fairfax, VA 22030-5647
703-691-3179

Lupus Foundation of America
4 Research Place, Suite 180
Rockville, MD 20850-3226
800-558-0121

National Foundation for Depressive Illness
P. O. Box 2257
New York, NY 10116
800-239-1265

PRODUCT PAGE

At The Body Advantage, we are pleased to offer you the following useful products. As distributors for the Miracle II products, we can make them available to you by contacting us.

Miracle II Soap

The versatility of these soaps is amazing. They are all natural, with no chemicals or harsh toxic agents. They have the potential to replace all your personal hair and skin products, as well as your household cleaning products. They possess the unique quality of being strong enough to disinfect, and gentle enough for your skin. Conveniently, the strength is determined by the amount used.

ACTIVE INGREDIENTS: Eloptic, energized, oxygenated water; ash of dedecyl solution; calcium; potassium; magnesium; foaming agent; laurel from the coconut.

Miracle II Moisturizing Soap

This amazing product represents a special blend of three Miracle II products. The soap, neutralizer and skin moisturizer are specially formulated into the moisturizing soap. It is the perfect replacement for all the chemical-filled and toxic products for your skin and hair care. No more commercial cleansing cremes and shampoos are needed. The special moisturizing soap contains no animal fat, synthetic oils or preservatives to clog the pores, and no deep-acting surfactants that strip the skin and hair of the nurturing natural oils within.

Miracle II Neutralizer

This neutralizer cleanses and detoxifies the blood as well as balances the pH to maintain an alkaline condition. Remember, bacteria, fungus, cancer cells and disease cannot exist where there is clear blood, a balanced pH, efficient elimination systems and a strong immune system. Add it to your water to aid thorough internal cleansing.

ACTIVE INGREDIENTS: Eloptic, energized, oxygenated water; ash of dedecyl solution; calcium; potassium and magnesium.

Miracle II Neutralizer Gel

The gel is formulated for those areas where one would like to maintain a high level of neutralizer for an extended period of time. The bottle is compact and portable and is convenient for mixing with your drinking water and for brushing your teeth. In addition, it serves as a skin repair lotion for cuts, burns and wounds, as well as for sunburn. Finally, it can also be used as a sunscreen.

Miracle II Skin Moisturizer

This moisturizer is used as an efficient replacement for skin cremes and lotions. It is excellent for dry skin and contains the same detoxifying benefits as the neutralizer. It contains incredible oils and emollients to feed the body and leave the skin baby soft and healthy. Men and women can use it as a shaving gel.

ACTIVE INGREDIENTS: Eloptic, energized, stabilized, oxygenated water; cold-pressed avocado; almond and coconut oils with vitamin E.

Miracle II Therapeutic and Laundry Ball

This is a rubber ball with 209 soft spikes impregnated with Miracle II soap and neutralizer. As a laundry ball it leaves your clothes and linens clean, refreshed, energized and free of chemical residual, not to be absorbed into your body to create toxic cells and eventually disease. The ball is also designed as therapeutic massage device to relax and energize the total body. The eloptic energy is released into the body for physical health benefits as well as a tool to help solve stress and depression problems.

OTHER RESOURCES FROM
THE BODY ADVANTAGE

The Body Advantage Exercise System

Developed by Dr. Joe M. Elrod, this truly unique piece of exercise equipment is designed to be one of the most comprehensive and effective wellness programs available on the market today. It has a wide range of uses for people of all ages and with every level of ability or disability. Originally designed for sufferers of fibromyalgia, arthritis and other systemic conditions to help regain flexibility, this system also helps the athlete and the average person seeking physical fitness by increasing strength, flexibility and neuromuscular coordination and control. Includes exercise device, twelve-week program guide, video and travel pouch.

The Success/Gratitude Journal

The Success/Gratitude Journal by Dr. Joe M. Elrod helps you identify your goals and create a plan for success. It includes planning charts and a daily log to track success and record the things you are thankful for, as well as other helpful information and inspirational tips.

The Fibromyalgia Nutrition Guide

This nutritional guide, by Mary Moeller, L.P.N. and Dr. Joe M. Elrod, contains valuable dietary guidelines, 150 recipes and more for overcoming fibromyalgia, chronic fatigue syndrome, migraines, sleep disorders and other chronic conditions.

Reversing Fibromyalgia

Reversing Fibromyalgia, the best-selling book by Dr. Joe M. Elrod, with over 300,000 copies sold worldwide, provides an alternative approach for overcoming fibromyalgia through nutrition, exercise, natural supplements and methods of coping with stress. It is one of the few resources that explains the cause of fibromyalgia and includes a successful reversal model.

The Body Advantage Twelve-Week Program Guide

This complete guide is designed in three phases and steps to take you by the hand to insure success as you pursue your healing pathway. Designed for you by Dr. Elrod to customize and personalize your program, it prepares you mentally, emotionally and spiritually to achieve your goals.

Patient Profile/ Health Risk Appraisal

The Patient Profile is a five-page medical and personal history form to provide information to assist in the analysis of your condition. You can request this form by e-mail, get it off the Internet at "thebodyadvantage.com" or write or call The Body Advantage office and request one.

Consultation

Schedule an appointment with Dr. Elrod either by phone or website to better assist you along your healing pathway.

E-mail your story to us or the story of a friend or your group. Thank you.

*For more information, including pricing and ordering information as well as information regarding consultations, seminars or speaking engagements,
please contact:*

Dr. Joe M. Elrod
117 Cedar Cove Dr.
Pelham, AL 35124
Phone: (205) 664-4553
Fax: (205) 664-4553
Toll free: 866-drelrod (373-5763)
E-mail: *drelrod@thebodyadvantage.com*
Website: *www.thebodyadvantage.com*